EYESALVE
A DAILY DEVOTIONAL WITH BIBLE READING SCHEDULE

By

Terry Fischer

This book has two purposes.

First, this book is a daily reading schedule of the Bible. If you follow the schedule you will read through the Old Testament once and the New Testament twice a year.

Second, there is a short comment given on a selected portion of scripture that is in every day's scheduled reading. These comments are what I call the "Eyesalve." The name Eyesalve is taken from Revelation 3:18 which says, *"I counsel thee to buy of me gold tried in the fire, that thou mayest be rich; and white raiment, that thou mayest be clothed, and that the shame of thy nakedness do not appear; and* **anoint thine eyes with eyesalve,** *that thou mayest see."*

This offer, to have their eyes anointed with salve, came from Jesus as He had John pen a letter to the Laodicean church about their lukewarm condition. The Lord still offers salve today for the eyes of anyone who desires to see the truth of His word. None of us will ever have to worry about being deceived, if we administer the eyesalve the Spirit of Truth gives to help us see and understand the word of God. Ask the Holy Spirit to give you that eyesalve and he will open your eyes to the deep truths of the Word of God. My Eyesalves are meant to be a little on the prophetic side, with a hint of sarcasm, so some readers may not appreciate the confronting and challenging tone of them. Of course, not every Eyesalve is like that. I assure you, they are written with the deepest love for God and His church. It is my intention to keep all Eyesalves short and to the point, however, it is not always that easy to do.

All scripture is taken from the King James Version of the Bible, unless it otherwise states. All bold type has been added by the author for emphasis.

First Printing in the fall of 2016

January

January 1
Read: Genesis 1-3; Matthew 1-2

Genesis 2:25, 3:7
"And they were both naked, the man and his wife, and were not ashamed......⁷And the eyes of them both were opened, and they knew that they were naked; and they sewed fig leaves together, and made themselves aprons."

When Adam and Eve had a right relationship with God they never felt any shame in their nakedness, but once their relationship with God was broken, shame enveloped their life. The shame which caused them to hide from God also caused them to hide their nakedness from each other. A strained relationship with God always results in a strained relationship between people, even with those you dearly love.

January 2
Read: Genesis 4-6; Matthew 3-4

Matthew 3:11
*"I indeed baptize you with water unto repentance: but he that cometh after me is mightier than I, whose shoes I am not worthy to bear: he shall baptize you with the Holy Ghost, and with **fire.**"*

This is John the Baptist's first recorded introduction of Jesus. Notice that he didn't say, "This one coming after me came to forgive you of your sins?" John didn't say, there is one coming who will deliver you or heal you or do great miracles. The first thing John said about Jesus was that He will baptize you with the Holy Ghost and fire. Hallelujah, church, you and I were saved to be filled with the Holy Ghost.

January 3
Read: Genesis 7-9; Matthew 5

Matthew 5:16
"Let your light so shine before men, that they may see your good works, and glorify your Father which is in heaven."

Light doesn't make noise or talk, it shines. Good works is not the light, the Spirit of God in you is. You are not just to let your light shine, but "let your light ***SO*** *shine.*" The word "so" means to a certain degree or impact. This means you are to be an attraction. Not an attraction to you, but to the Father.

January 4
Read: Genesis 10-12; Matthew 6

Matthew 6:9
"After this manner therefore pray ye: Our Father which art in heaven, Hallowed be thy name."

Jesus called the Father in heaven His Father. When His disciples asked Him to teach them to pray, the first thing He taught them was that they all had the same privilege as He did to call God Father. Hallelujah saints, He is "Our Father…"

January 5
Read: Genesis 13-15; Matthew 7

Genesis 14:21-23
"And the king of Sodom said unto Abram, 'Give me the persons, and take the goods to thyself.' ^{22}And Abram said to the king of Sodom, 'I have lift up mine hand unto the LORD, the most high God, the possessor of heaven and earth, ^{23}That I will not take from a thread even to a shoelatchet, and that I will not take any thing that is thine, lest thou shouldest say, I have made Abram rich.'"

You do not need one shoe latchet of help from this world to help you fulfill the call of God.

January 6
Read: Genesis 16-18; Matthew 8

Genesis 17:15-19
"And God said unto Abraham, As for Sarai thy wife, thou shalt not call her name Sarai, but Sarah shall her name be. ^{16}And I will bless her, and give thee a son also of her: yea, I will bless her, and she shall be a mother of nations; kings of people shall be of her. ^{17}Then Abraham fell upon his face, and laughed, and said in his heart, Shall a child be born unto him that is an hundred years old? and shall Sarah, that is ninety years old, bear? ^{18}And Abraham said unto God, O that Ishmael might live before thee! ^{19}And God said, Sarah thy wife shall bear thee a son indeed; and thou shalt call his name Isaac: and I will establish my covenant with him for an everlasting covenant, and with his seed after him."

When Abraham heard God tell him that his wife Sarah would have a son, Abraham for the moment found it easier to accept Ishmael as the one who would be the heir of God's promise. Too often we do the same thing. We settle for less than what God has for us. We find it easier to accept a place short of God's best than we do to believe Him for the fulfillment all His promises. In fact, God expects us to believe and receive all promises from Him. I know we are not to be a greedy people, but this is one time God wants us to go after it all.

January 7
Read: Genesis 19-20; Matthew 9

Genesis 20:6
*"And God said unto him in a dream, Yea, I know that thou didst this in the integrity of thy heart; for **I also withheld thee from sinning** against me: therefore suffered I thee not to touch her."*

If God will keep a heathen king from sinning against Him, imagine what he will do for you the born again believer.

January 8
Read: Genesis 21-22; Matthew 10

Genesis 21:4;
"*And Abraham circumcised his son Isaac being eight days old, as God had commanded him.*"

God wasn't looking for Isaac to have a missing foreskin; He was looking for Abraham to have an obedient heart. Abraham had an obedient heart and Isaac felt the effect of it. I pray that we all have such obedient hearts that are family and friends will feel the spiritual effect of it.

January 9
Read: Genesis 23-24; Matthew 11

Genesis 24:58
"*And they called Rebekah, and said unto her, Wilt thou go with this man? And she said, I will go.*"

Rebekah's family wanted her to delay her journey to meet her bridegroom, but they left it up to her. She decided to go, even though her family wanted her to wait for 10 days or so. Brethren, when it comes down to it, it is ultimately your decision if you are going after Jesus the bridegroom or not. No matter what family says, you must not delay your journey.

January 10
Read: Genesis 25-26; Matthew 12

Matthew 12:31-32
"*Wherefore I say unto you, All manner of sin and blasphemy shall be forgiven unto men: but the* **blasphemy against the Holy Ghost shall not be forgiven unto men**. *³²And whosoever speaketh a word against the Son of man, it shall be forgiven him: but whosoever speaketh against the Holy Ghost, it shall not be forgiven him, neither in this world, neither in the world to come.*"

The meaning of the word "blasphemy" means to vilify, which means to lower in estimation or importance. So when Jesus spoke about blasphemy against the Holy Ghost, He was saying that if you lower in estimation and the importance of the Holy Ghost, you are committing blasphemy against Him. I know here in America there are millions of so called Christians who have down played, ignored and even attributed the ministry of the Holy Ghost to Satan. Thank God that many of those who do that, do it in ignorance. Paul said he was *"before a blasphemer,"* but then he goes on to say, *but I obtained mercy, because I did it in ignorantly in unbelief."* (I Timothy 1:13). Saints, the Holy Ghost is God. Let's not be ignorant to the all-important ministry He does in the church and through the church. Do not take the path toward blasphemy.

January 11
Read: Genesis 27-28; Matthew 13

Matthew 13:11-12
"He answered and said unto them, Because it is given unto you to know the mysteries of the kingdom of heaven, but to them it is not given. **¹²*For whosoever hath, to him shall be given, and he shall have more abundance***: *but whosoever hath not, from him shall be taken away even that he hath."*

If you have ever wondered why you are growing in the Lord and getting greater revelation of the Lord (if you are), while you see other supposed Christians diminishing in their understanding of the Lord, it is because as the scriptures says, "to him who has they will be given more." These two scriptures are specifically talking about revelation of Christ. If you love the Lord and His word, and you sincerely seek Him, He will give you continual revelation of Himself, but those that are uninterested in knowing the Lord and just want salvation and have no desire to seek Him out, will eventually lose what revelation knowledge they have. As we close in on the remaining few years that are left before the Lord comes, you will see the gap grow. Those who diligently seek God will be receiving all that revelation in abundance; they will be getting that which is being taken from those that have other interests and desires. As the gap grows which side of the chasm will you be on?

January 12
Read: Genesis 29-30; Matthew 14

Genesis 29:20
"And Jacob served seven years for Rachel; and they seemed unto him but a few days, for the love he had to her."

Great love for someone keeps one preoccupied and content with life. During those many hours, days, weeks and months of laboring amongst the sheep, Jacob had his mind set on one person, Rachel. He was so excited about the coming day when he would be able to take this woman home to be his bride that he never got bogged down by anything. His heart was set and his eyes were looking ahead to that coming day. If you have a great love for the Lord and you are looking forward to that day when you will be with Him, this present age will seem but a few days because He will give you gladness of heart.

January 13
Read: Genesis 31; Matthew 15

Genesis 31:33-34
"And Laban went into Jacob's tent, and into Leah's tent, and into the two maidservants' tents; but he found them not. Then went he out of Leah's tent, and entered into Rachel's tent. ³⁴Now Rachel had taken the images, and put them in the camel's furniture, and sat upon them. And Laban searched all the tent, but found them not."

Go ahead Laban keep on searching, even if you find those images you have found no God. Hallelujah saints, we have the only God that promises that you will find Him when you search for Him with all your heart.

January 14
Read: Genesis 32-33; Matthew 16-17

Matthew 16:13-17
"When Jesus came into the coasts of Caesarea Philippi, he asked his

disciples, saying, Whom do men say that I the Son of man am? ¹⁴And they said, Some say that thou art John the Baptist: some, Elias; and others, Jeremias, or one of the prophets. ¹⁵He saith unto them, But whom say ye that I am? ¹⁶And Simon Peter answered and said, Thou art the Christ, the Son of the living God. ¹⁷And Jesus answered and said unto him, Blessed art thou, Simon Barjona: for flesh and blood hath not revealed it unto thee, but my Father which is in heaven."

Two words that you hear today in the Christian community are the words "relate" and "relevant." Ministers seem to be over concerned on how to relate to the people. Think about this; the omnipotent, omniscient, omnipresent, Almighty God made a way that He could relate to man and be relevant to mankind. He sent His Son to come and take human form to live amongst people in the very rigors and routine of life. He suffered trials, persecutions. He grew tired, hungry and thirsty. How about that for relevance? If you are one of those who are looking to relate to any age group, any class and any nationality of people, then preach the man, Christ Jesus.

January 15
Read: Genesis 34-35; Matthew 18

Genesis 34:1-2
"*And Dinah the daughter of Leah, which she bare unto Jacob, went out to **see** the daughters of the land. ²And when Shechem the son of Hamor the Hivite, prince of the country, saw her, he took her, and lay with her, **and defiled her**.*"

Dinah took an interest in the world. She did not go out looking for a boyfriend, she didn't go out to hit the mall; she just wanted to see the other ladies of the land, but the prince of that land saw her. It seemed innocent enough; but when she went out she was raped of her purity. She was defiled by the prince of this world. Saints of God, I must remind you over and over again, this world is not our friend. This is not our home. How dangerous it is, just to go out and see what it is like out there. We must forsake our every desire for it.

January 16
Read: Genesis 36-37; Matthew 19-20

Genesis 37:20
*"Come now therefore, and let us slay him, and cast him into some pit, and we will say, Some evil beast hath devoured him: and **we shall see what will become of his dreams**."*

Those dreams that Joseph had really bothered his brothers. They were afraid they would end up being true. So if they could kill him, it would put an end to his dreams. You know, you need to be careful who you share your dreams and promises from God with. There are plenty of skeptics out there that will put you down.

January 17
Read: Genesis 38-39; Matthew 21

Matthew 21:12-14
*"And Jesus went into the temple of God, and cast out all them that sold and bought in the temple, and overthrew the tables of the moneychangers, and the seats of them that sold doves, ^{13}And said unto them, It is written, My house shall be called the house of prayer; but ye have made it a den of thieves. ^{14}And the blind and the lame came to him in the temple; and **he healed them**."*

The hypocrites, pretenders and those who are in church for personal gain aren't so easy to get rid of. Jesus had to drive them out; but once they were removed, the healing power flowed. Saint of God, be a conduit at your church, not a resister.

January 18
Read: Genesis 40-41; Matthew 22

Genesis 41:14
Then Pharaoh sent and called Joseph, and they brought him hastily out of the dungeon: and he shaved himself, and changed his raiment, and came in unto Pharaoh.

Joseph woke up one morning in prison and went to bed in a palace. Kind of like the day a person becomes born again. They woke up a lost sinner going to hell and went to bed a redeemed saint, going to heaven.

January 19
Read: Genesis 42-44; Matthew 23-24

Matthew 24:1-2
"And Jesus went out, and departed from the temple: and his disciples came to him for to shew him the buildings of the temple. ²And Jesus said unto them, See ye not all these things? verily I say unto you, There shall not be left here one stone upon another, that shall not be thrown down."

No doubt that Jesus is prophesying here of the day when the temple would be destroyed, it happened a few decades later in 70 AD. But there is something else that can be gleaned from these verses. The disciples had pointed out to Jesus the pride of Israel, the great temple. It represents what men have achieved. It represented their little place in this world; *"...the pride of life...* (I Jn. 2:16). Jesus immediately declared, it will come down. That still stands true today. Anything we exalt in this world, any sense of pride in our earthly accomplishments, anything we point out and commend ourselves for, Jesus stands against it and says it will be thrown down.

January 20
Read: Genesis 45-46; Matthew 25

Matthew 25:20, 28
"And so he that had received five talents came and brought other five talents, saying, Lord, thou deliveredst unto me five talents: behold, I have gained beside them five talents more...²⁸Take therefore the talent from him, and give it unto him which hath ten talents.

The man in verse twenty was once known as, *"he that had received five talents."* The man in verse twenty eight is the same man from verse twenty, he has just taken on a new identity. He is now called, *"him which hath ten talents."* If we are growing and being blessed, then we will also take on a new identity.

January 21
Read: Genesis 47-48; Matthew 26

Matthew 26:35
"Peter said unto him, Though I should die with thee, yet will I not deny thee. Likewise also said all the disciples."

Man's natural zeal never holds up. This is made evident through the Apostle Peter. He was quick to shoot his mouth off that he would even be willing to die for his master, yet when the pressure came, he bailed out and denied even knowing Jesus. This is why it is so important and necessary for the Christian to receive the baptism of the Holy Ghost and fire. Man's fire burns out, God's fire is sustained by the oil of the Holy Ghost. The Spirit of God never diminishes nor does He grow weary. He can be grieved but He does not get timid. The days are upon us when this world is looking to eliminate those who love God. They might come to you and say, *"Surely thou also art one of them* (26:73)." First of all, will you be recognized as being one of them? Secondly, will you have the courage to admit it? The baptism of fire will take you through it all. Ask the Lord to baptize you with the Spirit and fire and start burning for Him. Hallelujah!

January 22
Read: Genesis 49-50; Matthew 27:1-44

Genesis 50:20
"But as for you, you meant evil against me; but God meant it for good, in order to bring it about as it is this day, to save many people alive."

God never does evil toward His children, but He does allow it to happen. When it does happen to you, be confident that God is going to do something really good through it.

January 23
Read: Exodus 1-3; Matthew 27:45 - 28

Exodus 2:11-14
"And it came to pass in those days, when Moses was grown, that he went out unto his brethren, and looked on their burdens: and he spied an Egyptian smiting an Hebrew, one of his brethren. [12]And he looked this way and that way, and when he saw that there was no man, he slew the Egyptian, and hid him in the sand. [13]And when he went out the second day, behold, two men of the Hebrews strove together: and he said to him that did the wrong, Wherefore smitest thou thy fellow? [14]And he said, Who made thee a prince and a judge over us? intendest thou to kill me, as thou killedst the Egyptian? And Moses feared, and said, Surely this thing is known."

Moses saw the injustice and had it in his heart to do something about it. He decided that killing the Egyptian was the best option. However, that was not God's plan. Seeing the need and bondage of mankind is not the call to reach them, rather the call is realized as you get to know the Lord, share His burden and follow His orders. Then you can go and see the burning bush. It won't do the kingdom of God any good for you to be out there smiting Egyptians.

January 24
Read: Exodus 4-6; Mark 1

Exodus 4:20
*"And Moses took his wife and his sons, and set them upon an ass, and he returned to the land of Egypt: and Moses took the **rod of God** in his hand."*

In the backside of the wilderness, the stick in Moses hand was a staff for shepherding sheep. When the call of God came upon Moses, that staff became the rod of God. If a mere shepherd's staff can become the rod of God, imagine what you could become for God.

January 25
Read: Exodus 7-8; Mark 2

Mark 2:3-5
"And they come unto him, bringing one sick of the palsy, which was borne of four. ⁴And when they could not come nigh unto him for the press, they uncovered the roof where he was: and when they had broken it up, they let down the bed wherein the sick of the palsy lay. ⁵When Jesus saw their faith, he said unto the sick of the palsy, Son, thy sins be forgiven thee."

I don't know for sure if the man sick with the palsy had faith to be healed, but those men who carried him did. *"Jesus saw **their** faith."* You could see these men's faith by their works. It was a faith that was alive that caused these men to do whatever it took to get their friend to Jesus, and this living faith healed the palsy as well. Hallelujah!

January 26
Read: Exodus 9-10; Mark 3

Exodus 9:13-14
*"And the LORD said unto Moses, Rise up early in the morning, and stand before Pharaoh, and say unto him, Thus saith the LORD God of the Hebrews, Let my people go, that they may serve me. ¹⁴For I will at this time send all my plagues upon thine heart, and upon thy servants, and upon thy people; **that thou mayest know that there is none like me in all the earth.**"*

I am tired of a Christianity that has no distinction from all the other religions. Too often, Christianity is looked at as just another religion to pick from. Christianity should be unlike any religion in this world. Christians are the only ones who have a Risen Lord. They are the only ones who have a spiritual birth. They are the only ones who can take on the very image of their God, but yet the rest of the world sees Christianity as just another religion to pick from. God told Moses to rise early in the morning and go speak for Him in the presence of Pharaoh and say, *"Let My people go..."* So Moses rose early and put his neck on the line and spoke up for God. Now it was God's turn to come through, which we know He did. God sent Moses not just to lead the Israelites out of Egypt into God's blessing, but that God could also make a name for Himself all over the earth, *"That thou mayest know that there is **none like me in all the earth**."* If this world can once again see that there is no God like our God, then they will see that Christianity is not just like any other religion.

January 27
Read: Exodus 11-12; Mark 4

Exodus 12:23
"For the LORD will pass through to smite the Egyptians; and when he seeth the blood upon the lintel, and on the two side posts, the LORD will pass over the door, and will not suffer the destroyer to come in unto your houses to smite you."

Saints, here is the power and wonder of the blood. When that death angel went through Egypt he did not knock on the door of the houseswith blood on them to see if everyone inside was behaving. He did not stop in to make sure that every person was living right; he just passed on by because of the blood. This is our comfort as well. The blood of Jesus keeps us in right standing with God, otherwise we would be going in and out of salvation every time we sinned. However, to remain protected you have to stay in the house. You have to stay in Christ. You can't go looking out the door, for if you start looking out there to see what's going on, you will eventually go out there to be a part of it. If you come out from behind the blood you are in big trouble. Stay in the house, abide in the VINE.

January 28
Read: Exodus 13-14; Mark 5

Mark 5:18-20
"And when he was come into the ship, he that had been possessed with the devil prayed him that he might be with him. [19]Howbeit Jesus suffered him not, but saith unto him, Go home to thy friends, and tell them how great things the Lord hath done for thee, and hath had compassion on thee. [20]And he departed, and began to publish in

Decapolis how great things Jesus had done for him: and all men did marvel."

When you get saved you don't need to go through evangelism classes, you don't need to go to a work shop on how to win souls. The demoniac who used to run around naked, who had such strong demonic power that he could break chains, had an encounter with Jesus. When Jesus got done with him, he was clothed and in the right mind. This demoniac was now armed with one of the most powerful soul winning tools; he had a testimony. He wanted to go with Jesus but Jesus commissioned him to, *"Go home to thy friends, and tell them how great things the Lord hath done for thee."* It may take years of study and prayer to show yourself approved to fulfill a call to the five-fold ministry, but when it comes to soul winning (if you are born again) you have a testimony, and if you have a testimony then you can go and tell others what great things God has done for you. Then men can marvel.

January 29
Read: Exodus 15-16; Mark 6

Exodus 16:15-20
"And when the children of Israel saw it, they said one to another, It is manna: for they wist not what it was. And Moses said unto them, **This is the bread which the LORD hath given you to eat.** *^{16}This is the thing which the LORD hath commanded, Gather of it every man according to his eating, an omer for every man, according to the number of your persons; take ye every man for them which are in his tents. ^{17}And the children of Israel did so, and gathered, some more, some less. ^{18}And when they did mete it with an omer, he that gathered much had nothing over, and he that gathered little had no lack; they gathered every man according to his eating. ^{19}And Moses said, Let no man leave of it till the morning. ^{20}Notwithstanding they hearkened not unto Moses; but some of them left of it until the morning,* **and it bred worms, and stank***: and Moses was wroth with them."*

The manna that fell for the Israelites to eat is a type of Christ. This manna fell with a condition. They were to gather up just what they needed for the day. However, some of those rebellious Israelites disobeyed what the Lord had commanded and gathered more. The results were the manna *"bred worms, and stank."* It is the same thing with a religion where the people profess they have Jesus the bread of life, yet they live in disobedience. They have nothing but a religion that stinks. It doesn't breed sheep, it breeds worms.

January 30
Read: Exodus 17-18; Mark 7

Exodus 17:6
"Behold, I will stand before thee there upon the rock in Horeb; and thou shalt smite the rock, and there shall come water out of it, that the people may drink. And Moses did so in the sight of the elders of Israel."

The rock was struck and the water flowed *"That the people may drink."* Christ the Rock was smitten and life flows for all today who will drink.

January 31
Read: Exodus 19-20; Mark 8

Exodus 20:25
*"And if thou wilt make me an altar of stone, thou shalt not build it of hewn stone: for if thou lift up thy tool upon it, **thou hast polluted it**."*

Our generation needs to quit reshaping the church; we need to quit trying to chisel out a new Christianity. With it comes pollution and polluted water brings death and disease.

February

February 1
Read: Exodus 21-22; Mark 9

Mark 9:11-13
"And they asked him, saying, Why say the scribes that Elias must first come? ¹²And he answered and told them, Elias verily cometh first, and restoreth all things; and how it is written of the Son of man, that he must suffer many things, and be set at nought. ¹³But I say unto you, That Elias is indeed come, and they have done unto him whatsoever they listed, as it is written of him."

The Elias who came that Jesus is referring to is John the Baptist. If a person doesn't have spiritual eyes to see spiritual things, all they will see is the flesh. And so it was in the case of John the Baptist. When looking at John, Jesus saw that Elijah came; when the people saw John, they just saw the man John.

February 2
Read: Exodus 23-25; Mark 10

Exodus 25:21-22
"And thou shalt put the mercy seat above upon the ark; and in the ark thou shalt put the testimony that I shall give thee. ²²And there I will meet with thee, and I will commune with thee from above the mercy seat, from between the two cherubims which are upon the ark of the testimony, of all things which I will give thee in commandment unto the children of Israel."

God's first intention toward man is to look down upon mankind through the eyes of mercy. Thank you Lord for that. Thank you Lord that you prefer mercy over wrath.

February 3
Read: Exodus 26-27; Mark 11

Exodus 27:20
"And thou shalt command the children of Israel, that they bring thee pure oil olive beaten for the light, to cause the lamp to burn always."

When the children of Israel kept bringing the oil, the lamp kept on burning. If they didn't it would go out. If we keep on obeying the Lord, our lamp burns bright, if we don't it burns out. No obedience, no Holy Ghost fire.

February 4
Read: Exodus 28; Mark 12

Exodus 28:36-38
"And thou shalt make a plate of pure gold, and grave upon it, like the engravings of a signet, HOLINESS TO THE LORD. ³⁷And thou shalt put it on a blue lace, that it may be upon the mitre; upon the forefront of the mitre it shall be. ³⁸And it shall be upon Aaron's forehead, that Aaron may bear the iniquity of the holy things, which the children of Israel shall hallow in all their holy gifts; and it shall be always upon his forehead, that they may be accepted before the LORD."

Aaron had to wear a sign on his forehead that said, "HOLINESS TO THE LORD." When God changed covenants from the old to the new, He put "HOLINESS TO THE LORD" on the inside of man. You don't wear holiness, you walk in holiness.

February 5
Read: Exodus 29-30; Mark 13

Exodus 30:37-38
"And as for the perfume which thou shalt make, **ye shall not make to yourselves according to the composition thereof: it shall be unto thee holy for the LORD**. *³⁸Whosoever shall make like unto that, to smell thereto, shall even be cut off from his people."*

Does God take pleasure in smelling perfume? It isn't the smell of the perfume that God desires. He smells the obedience, He smells holiness and He smells consecration and dedication. Brethren, we don't need perfume and cologne to make us smell good before God; obedience, holiness, consecration and dedication work just fine and if you continue therein, it won't wear off either.

February 6
Read: Exodus 31-32; Mark 14

Mark 14:1
"After two days was the feast of the passover, and of unleavened bread: and the chief priests and the scribes sought how they might **take him by craft***, and put him to death."*

Since they could not find anything that Jesus did wrong, the chief priests and the scribes had to make up lies about Him so they could have Him arrested. Next time someone falsely accuses you, rejoice that it is not true; rejoice they couldn't find you doing any wrong.

February 7
Read: Exodus 33-34; Mk. 15

Exodus 34:29-30
"And it came to pass, when Moses came down from mount Sinai with the two tables of testimony in Moses' hand, when he came down from the mount, that Moses wist not that the skin of his face shone while he talked with him. ³⁰And when Aaron and all the children of Israel saw Moses, behold, the skin of his face shone; **and they were afraid to come nigh him***."*

Do you want God to talk more clearly to you, yet it seems He won't respond? Look at Israel, when they could get a close-up look at the glory of the Lord that was on Moses' face, they backed away. They were afraid to really see God; could it be you are really afraid to hear God? Could it be that deep in your heart there is a fear of hearing God, because then you would have to respond in obedience? Maybe the issue is not if God's willing to talk to you, but if you are willing to obey Him when He does

February 8
Read: Exodus 35-36; Mark 16

Exodus 36:6-7
"And Moses gave commandment, and they caused it to be proclaimed throughout the camp, saying, Let neither man nor woman make any more work for the offering of the sanctuary. So the people were restrained from bringing. ⁷For the stuff they had was sufficient for all the work to make it, and too much."

I recently heard that one of these rich popular preachers asked his church to help make him a billionaire. I've noticed these prosperity preachers are no different than the rich people of this world, they can never seem to get enough money. Well, they need to know that even God said there was no more need to collect any more offerings. He even said what came in was already *"too much."* If you are content with Christ, then what you have is sufficient. If you are not content with Christ, then you can never have enough.

February 9
Read: Exodus 37-38; Luke 1:1-40

Luke 1:15
"For he shall be great in the sight of the Lord, and shall drink neither wine nor strong drink; and he shall be filled with the Holy Ghost, even from his mother's womb."

Wine and strong drink are not compatible with the Holy Ghost.

February 10
Read: Exodus 39-40; Luke 1:41-80

Exodus 39:43
"And Moses did look upon all the work, and, behold, they had done it as the LORD had commanded, even so had they done it: and Moses blessed them."

How refreshing it is to read when once in a while the people obeyed God. It states it so simple, they did the work as the Lord commanded, *"even so had they done it."* No complaining, no fighting over who does what, no excuses, no laziness, just setting their mind to do as the Lord commanded. After that the blessing came. Oh, for the day the church will obey God again.

February 11
Read: Leviticus 1-3; Luke 2

Leviticus 3:1
"And if his oblation be a sacrifice of peace offering, if he offer it of the herd; whether it be a male or female, he shall offer it without blemish before the LORD."

Religion focuses on the sacrifice and the offering; a relationship with Christ is concerned more about not having a defect or blemish.

February 12
Read: Leviticus 4-5; Luke 3

Luke 3:7-8
"Then said he to the multitude that came forth to be baptized of him, O generation of vipers, who hath warned you to flee from the wrath to come? ⁸Bring forth therefore fruits worthy of repentance, and begin not to say within yourselves, We have Abraham to our father: for I say unto you, That God is able of these stones to raise up children unto Abraham."

Stones are softer than the hard hearts of men.

February 13
Read: Leviticus 6-7; Luke 4

Luke 4:14
"And Jesus returned in the power of the Spirit into Galilee: and there went out a fame of him through all the region round about."

Jesus left Galilee a perfect man and returned to Galilee a perfect Spirit filled man. How we need the church to return *"in the power of the Spirit."* How we need the church to return to her roots of Holy Spirit power and authority. Saints, please pray and believe for this.

February 14
Read: Leviticus 8-9; Luke 5

Leviticus 9:7
"And Moses said unto Aaron, Go unto the altar, and offer thy sin offering, and thy burnt offering, and **make an atonement for thyself, and for the people***: and offer the offering of the people, and make an atonement for them; as the LORD command*ed."

Christians run into trouble with other Christians when they focus on other people first. They point their finger at others, but have neglected to get their own life right with the Lord first. Moses set the example with Aaron when he told him *"Make atonement for thyself.."* After that then Aaron could make atonement for the people. Once that beam is gone from our own eye, then we can help our brothers and sisters deal with their speck.

February 15
Read: Leviticus 10-11; Luke 6

Luke 6:38
"**Give***, and it shall be given unto you; good measure, pressed down, and shaken together, and running over, shall men give into your bosom. For with the same measure that ye mete withal it shall be measured to you again."*

Oh, how those words "*...running over, shall men give into your bosom,*" are so loved. But you never get to the reality of those words unless you embrace the first word of the verse, "*Give.*"

February 16
Read: Leviticus 12-13; Luke 7

Leviticus 13:44-46
"*He is a leprous man, he is unclean: the priest shall pronounce him utterly unclean; his plague is in his head. ⁴⁵And the leper in whom the plague is, his clothes shall be rent, and his head bare, and he shall put a covering upon his upper lip, and shall cry,* **Unclean, unclean.** *⁴⁶All the days wherein the plague shall be in him he shall be defiled; he is unclean:* **he shall dwell alone; without the camp shall his habitation be.**"

The law of leprosy required that the leper was to put a covering over his upper lip and cry, "*unclean, unclean.*" If that wasn't bad enough just to have leprosy, you had to shout it out to everyone. Then that leper was banished from the camp and was to live the remainder of his life shut away from all he loves, unless he was healed. I can imagine what joy a person healed from leprosy would have. They would be able to come back to the household of their family and partake in all that the family does. That first meal together would be the tastiest. The first embrace and kiss would be the sweetest. There would be a great celebration going on. Yet, Christians have been healed of a plague much more severe and chronic than leprosy. I wonder where all the celebrating is. I wonder why so many frowns. I wonder why so many heavy burdens. Church, we have been made clean by the blood of the Lamb. We took a bath in that fountain and have come away clean before a holy God. Our life once shouted unclean, unclean. Now we have been made pure. I think that calls for a celebration.

February 17
Read: Leviticus 14; Luke 8

Luke 8:15
*"But that on the good ground are they, which in an honest and good heart, having heard the word, keep it, and **bring forth fruit with patience**."*

We learn from Luke that good ground and the word of God bring forth fruit in our life. However, patience is what gives fruit time to grow. The word patience means, endurance and constancy. The word, when it is planted in your heart, will do its work if you continue to endure and be constant about the things of God. Go faithfully about God's business in your life and watch the fruit spring forth.

February 18
Read: Leviticus 15-16; Luke 9

Luke 9:23
"And he said to them all, If any man will come after me, let him deny himself, and take up his cross daily, and follow me."

There are two aspects of the cross, one is the cross of Christ which is salvation and the other is your cross that you must *"take up."* If you want the crowds, just preach the salvation side of the cross; if you want disciples for the Lord, preach the *"take up"* side of the cross.

February 19
Read: Leviticus 17-18; Luke 10

Leviticus 18:2-5
*"Speak unto the children of Israel, and say unto them, I am the LORD your God. ³**After the doings of the land of Egypt, wherein ye dwelt, shall ye not do: and after the doings of the land of Canaan, whither I bring you, shall ye not do: neither shall ye walk in their ordinances. ⁴Ye shall do my judgments, and keep mine ordinances, to walk therein:** I am the LORD your God".*

There is a life of sin we have left behind. There is an Egypt we have come out of. We must forget those things which are behind; never to long for that old life again. Though we left that world, it still is there to tempt us. It is nothing different, it is the same old system we got delivered from. No matter what you have come out of, no matter what lies ahead, there is a Lord we must obey. It is His kingdom that we now walk in. That kingdom is wherever you take it. You left Egypt to walk in the kingdom of God, and that kingdom cannot be thwarted by any world that lies before you. If you walk faithful and obey God's ordinances, you will be firmly planted in God's unshakable kingdom. Hallelujah!

February 20
Read: Leviticus 19-20; Luke 11

Luke 11:33
"No man, when he hath lighted a candle, putteth it in a secret place, neither under a bushel, but on a candlestick, that they which come in may see the light."

God lights us. We are His lamp. All we have to do is burn.

February 21
Read: Leviticus 21-22; Luke 12

Luke 12:34
"For where your treasure is, there will your heart be also."

If your treasure is Christ, your heart will follow after Christ alone and find Him all sufficient. If your treasure isn't Christ, your life will be clogged up with many other things. What is in your treasure chest?

February 22
Read: Leviticus 23-24; Luke 13

Leviticus 23:8
***"But ye shall offer an offering made by fire unto the LORD** seven days: in the seventh day is an holy convocation: ye shall do no servile work therein."*

You are the offering; make sure you let the refiner's fire deal with you.

February 23
Read: Leviticus 25; Luke 14

Luke 14:16-20
"Then said he unto him, A certain man made a great supper, and bade many: ^{17}And sent his servant at supper time to say to them that were bidden, Come; for all things are now ready. ^{18}And they all with one consent began to make excuse. The first said unto him, I have bought a piece of ground, and I must needs go and see it: I pray thee have me excused. ^{19}And another said, I have bought five yoke of oxen, and I go to prove them: I pray thee have me excused. ^{20}And another said, I have married a wife, and therefore I cannot come."

One man said, "*I needs go,*" another said, "*I go to prove*" and yet another said, "*I cannot come.*" Really when it comes down to it, they all were saying, "I will not come, I am to busy for You." God has always had a harder time with those who are too busy for Him than He has had with lost sinners of this world.

February 24
Read: Leviticus 26-27; Luke 15-16

Leviticus 26:3-6
"If ye walk in my statutes, and keep my commandments, and do them; ^{4}Then I will give you rain in due season, and the land shall yield her increase, and the trees of the field shall yield their fruit. ^{5}And your threshing shall reach unto the vintage, and the vintage

shall reach unto the sowing time: and ye shall eat your bread to the full, and dwell in your land safely. ⁶And I will give peace in the land, and ye shall lie down, and none shall make you afraid: and I will rid evil beasts out of the land, neither shall the sword go through your land."

The teachers from the word of faith camp will tell you that if you obey God then He has to bless you. They insist that if you are not being blessed then you are not right with God. We read that God does say if we obey His statutes and commandments that He will give us rain, food to eat and land to dwell safely in. There is no one who knows that better than a Christian who lives in America. However, if you are living for God and things turn for the worse and your daily provision becomes scarce and you would even lose your land, does that mean that God has failed to keep His word? Absolutely not, it just means you are feeling the weight of your cross. And He is just preparing you for something even better than all of that stuff.

February 25
Read: Numbers 1-2; Luke 17

Luke 17:26-30
"And as it was in the days of Noe, so shall it be also in the days of the Son of man. ²⁷They did eat, they drank, they married wives, they were given in marriage, until the day that Noe entered into the ark, and the flood came, and destroyed them all. ²⁸Likewise also as it was in the days of Lot; they did eat, they drank, they bought, they sold, they planted, they builded; ²⁹But the same day that Lot went out of Sodom it rained fire and brimstone from heaven, and destroyed them all. ³⁰Even thus shall it be in the day when the Son of man is revealed."

There are two things we can learn from the above passages that are referring to these last days. One is that life will go on as usual. That does not mean that there won't be financial problems happening; it does not mean that there will not be disasters taking place in this world. For the most part, the world as a whole will be living the way that has been common to man throughout history. The second thing that makes my heart leap is that Noah and Lot were removed before that destruction came. Noah and Lot represent the church. The church will be removed before the wrath of God is poured out on this world. Hallelujah, are you ready to go?

February 26
Read: Numbers 3-4; Luke 18

Numbers 3:38
"But those that encamp before the tabernacle toward the east, even before the tabernacle of the congregation eastward, shall be Moses, and Aaron and his sons, keeping the charge of the sanctuary for the charge of the children of Israel; ***and the stranger that cometh nigh shall be put to death.****"*

I am not suggesting putting anyone to death, but am just pointing out the severity it is for someone who is a stranger to God to think they can enter God's sanctuary (church) and worship Him with the other saints without repentance. Making it even more personal, have you been a stranger to God all week and then entered His sanctuary as if you haven't been?

February 27
Read: Numbers 5-6; Luke 19

Luke 19:2-5
"And, behold, there was a man named Zacchaeus, which was the chief among the publicans, and he was rich. ³And he sought to see Jesus who he was; and could not for the press, because he was little of stature. ⁴And he ran before, and climbed up into a sycomore tree to see him: for he was to pass that way. ⁵And when Jesus came to the place, he looked up, and saw him, and said unto him, Zacchaeus, make haste, and come down; for today I must abide at thy house."

It is when you press on to see Jesus that He will see you. He will know who you are too.

February 28 & 29
Read: Numbers 7; Luke 20

Numbers 7:1
"Now it came to pass, when Moses had finished setting up the tabernacle, that he anointed it and **consecrated it** *and all its furnishings, and the altar and all its utensils; so* **he anointed them** *and consecrated them."*

One terrible disservice that is done by the leaders of our churches is that they anoint men to the ministry before they are ever consecrated for the work. We must first be set apart before we can ever receive the anointing from God.

Luke 20:4-6
"The baptism of John, was it from heaven, or of men? ⁵And they reasoned with themselves, saying, If we shall say, From heaven; he will say, Why then believed ye him not? ⁶But and if we say, Of men; all the people will stone us: for they be persuaded that John was a prophet."

The people were persuaded that John was a prophet. Their persuasion was correct. It is no different today than it was in the days of Jesus. We have many religious leaders who don't have the persuasion that the people have. They don't have the revelation that the people have. Saints of God, pray that the Lord will raise up strong godly spiritual leaders in this closing hour who will be persuaded of the word of God.

March

March 1
Read: Numbers 8-9; Luke 21

Luke 21:34
*"And take heed to yourselves, lest at any time your hearts be overcharged with surfeiting, and drunkenness, and **cares of this life**, and so that day come upon you unawares."*

It is apparent that a Christian's heart can be overcome with the cares of life to such a point that the day of the Lord can catch them by surprise. The cares of life are different than sinful things. You can avoid sin; you can avoid those things that can cause temptation. Joseph ran from Potiphar's wife when she came tempting him. However, the cares of life you cannot run from, they are ever before you if you are a responsible Christian. YOU DO NOT AVOID THE CARES OF LIFE, YOU OVERCOME THEM.

March 2
Read: Numbers 10; Luke 22

Luke 22:51
"And Jesus answered and said, Suffer ye thus far. And he touched his ear, and healed him."

A better translation for the words, *"Suffer ye thus far"* is, *"permit even this"* (NKJV). Our natural reaction to every trial and tribulation is to resist it and beg God to deliver us, but many times we need to *"permit even this."* Even your worst situation? Yes, even that. God is perfecting you. Permitting is perfecting.

March 3
Read: Numbers 11; Luke 23

Numbers 11:4-6
"And the mixt multitude that was among them fell a lusting: and the children of Israel also wept again, and said, Who shall give us flesh to eat? ⁵We remember the fish, which we did eat in Egypt freely; the cucumbers, and the melons, and the leeks, and the onions, and the garlick: ⁶But now our soul is dried away: there is nothing at all, beside this manna, before our eyes."

Let me paraphrase verse six to sound like the way the Lord heard their cry. "But now our soul is unsatisfied because there is nothing but these lousy provisions You, Lord, have given us." That is how the Lord hears any complaining.

March 4
Read: Numbers 12-13; Luke 24

Numbers 13:30-31
*"And Caleb stilled the people before Moses, and said, **Let us go up at once**, and possess it; for we are well able to overcome it. ³¹But the men that went up with him said, **We be not able to go** up against the people; for they are stronger than we."*

Caleb said *"Let us go at once,.."* but the other men said, *"We be not able to go."* So they did not go and those men died in the wilderness. Jesus told our generation, *"Go ye therefore, and teach all nations,…"* Let us not dare say, *"We be not able to go."*

March 5
Read: Numbers 14-15; John 1

Numbers 14:1-2, 5
*"And all the congregation lifted up their voice, and cried; and the people wept that night. ²And all the children of Israel **murmured against Moses and against Aaron**: and the whole congregation said unto them, Would God that we had died in the land of Egypt! or*

would God we had died in this wilderness... ⁵Then **Moses and Aaron fell on their faces** *before all the assembly of the congregation of the children of Israel."*

If you mourn and grieve over lost sinners, you will not be so easily offended by them, you will instead intercede for them.

March 6
Read: Numbers 16-17; John 2-3

John 3:21
"But he that doeth truth cometh to the light, that his deeds may be made manifest, that they are wrought in God."

The believer must make truth the priority of his life. Living in truth keeps the light shining bright. And when the light is bright, the believer can see his way and will not be deceived. If you allow the truth to diminish in your life, your way will grow dark. Soon the works and manifestation of God will decrease in your life, unless you once again subject yourself to the whole truth. You must walk in the whole truth not just a part of it.

Extra:
John 3:30
"He must increase, but I must decrease."

There is no better way to overcome the flesh than by continually seeking the Lord and allowing His life to increase in you. As His life increases in you, it will push out all that isn't Christ and thus your flesh will decrease. Hallelujah!

March 7
Read: Numbers 18-19; John 4

John 4:20-24
"Our fathers worshipped in this mountain; and ye say, that in Jerusalem is the place where men ought to worship. ²¹Jesus saith unto her, Woman, believe me, the hour cometh, when ye shall neither

in this mountain, nor yet at Jerusalem, worship the Father. ^{22}Ye worship ye know not what: we know what we worship: for salvation is of the Jews. ^{23}But the hour cometh, and now is, when the true worshippers shall worship the Father in spirit and in truth: for the Father seeketh such to worship him. ^{24}God is a Spirit: and they that worship him must worship him in spirit and in truth."

True worship isn't on a mountain in Samaria or even in Jerusalem. True worship isn't in a place called a church. True worship is a condition of the heart and a life that is lived. When you walk in the Spirit and abide in the truth, then you live a life that worships God, whether in church or on a mountain. The Father doesn't seek out singers and musicians, though they are nice to have, He seeks for those who worship Him in spirit and truth.

March 8
Read: Numbers 20-21; John 5

Numbers 20:10-12
"And Moses and Aaron gathered the congregation together before the rock, and he said unto them, Hear now, ye rebels; must we fetch you water out of this rock? ^{11}And Moses lifted up his hand, and with his rod he smote the rock twice: and the water came out abundantly, and the congregation drank, and their beasts also. ^{12}And the LORD spake unto Moses and Aaron, Because ye believed me not, to sanctify me in the eyes of the children of Israel, therefore ye shall not bring this congregation into the land which I have given them."

Moses disobeyed God, yet God still caused water to flow from the rock. This goes to show that just because God does a miracle for us, it doesn't necessarily mean we are doing His will.

March 9
Read: Numbers 22-23; John 6

Numbers 22:5
"He sent messengers therefore unto Balaam the son of Beor to Pethor, which is by the river of the land of the children of his people,

*to call him, saying, **Behold, there is a people come out from Egypt: behold, they cover the face of the earth, and they abide over against me.***"

Balak the prophet was scared stiff because there were some people, God's people, who were heading his way coming out of Egypt. If the church today would once and for all come out of Egypt, she would have the same impact as well.

March 10
Read: Numbers 24-25; John 7

John 7:38
"He that believeth on me, as the scripture hath said, out of his belly shall flow rivers of living water."

If living water does not flow from our bellies, then just mere words will flow from our mind out our mouths.

March 11
Read: Numbers 26; John 8

Numbers 26:63-65
"These are they that were numbered by Moses and Eleazar the priest, who numbered the children of Israel in the plains of Moab by Jordan near Jericho. ⁶⁴But among these there was not a man of them whom Moses and Aaron the priest numbered, when they numbered the children of Israel in the wilderness of Sinai. ⁶⁵For the LORD had said of them, They shall surely die in the wilderness. And there was not left a man of them, save Caleb the son of Jephunneh, and Joshua the son of Nun."

Israel was approaching the end of their journey through the wilderness. They have wandered for nearly forty years. There is something they left behind; in fact they left thousands of this one thing behind; it was grave markers. Somewhere scattered across the wilderness there were stones that testified that rebels were buried there. They believed the bad report of the ten spies and therefore

God swore they shall not enter in. So this era had finished, those doubters all died off and Israel is preparing to take the land. In like manner, Christians must go forward to the deeper life in Christ. There is one of two choices that can be made, one is to go forward and have a living testimony or the other is to refuse to go forward in the Lord and have a grave marker as your testimony.

March 12
Read: Numbers 27-28; John 9

John 9:5
"As long as I am in the world, I am the light of the world."

If there is going to be light in this world, Christ has to be in it. If Christ is going to be in this world, He has to be in you, He has to be in His church.

March 13
Read: Numbers 29-30; John 10

John 10:10
"The thief cometh not, but for to steal, and to kill, and to destroy: I am come that they might have life, and that they might have it more abundantly."

What a contrast between Jesus and the devil. The devil offers complete destruction while Jesus offers abundant life. Notice there is no middle ground! Christians should not be just getting by another day, they should not live a ho-hum existence. I am not denying that we will face trials, but it is only a believer who can, in the midst of a trial, be living an abundant life. The reason is because Jesus is our abundant life. If a billionaire was thrown in jail for twenty years, would he still not have his billions of dollars? So too, if a believer is under persecution, does he have any less of Jesus?

March 14
Read: Numbers 31-32; John 11

John 11:32
"Then when Mary was come where Jesus was, and saw him, she fell down at his feet, saying unto him, Lord, if thou hadst been here, my brother had not died."

Mary believed Jesus could have healed Lazarus, but Jesus wanted her to believe He can raise him from the dead. God wants us to believe Him for the impossible. God is always busy revealing to us just how great He is.

March 15
Read: Numbers 33-34; John 12

Numbers 33:55
"But if ye will not drive out the inhabitants of the land from before you; then it shall come to pass, that those which ye let remain of them shall be pricks in your eyes, and thorns in your sides, and shall vex you in the land wherein ye dwell."

In the Old Testament days, the Israelites were to kill the inhabitants of the Promised Land so they would not be a snare to them. In this age of grace we must not do such a thing. We have no choice but to live amongst the prickles and thorns in this society. We don't kill them, we overcome them. *"Ye are of God, little children, and have overcome them: because greater is he that is in you, than he that is in the world"* (I John 4:4).

March 16
Read: Numbers 35-36; John 13

John 13:34
"A new commandment I give unto you, That ye love one another; as I have loved you, that ye also love one another."

To love one another is not a new commandment, for God required that from days of old. What is new however, is the example of what real love is. Before Christ, there was no perfect example of true love. True love is a love that causes someone to deny themselves for the sake of others. Jesus had this perfect love. He died for those who spat on Him, mocked Him and crucified Him. It wasn't just those religious leaders who demanded Him to be crucified, but you and I were just as guilty as they. So there is our perfect pattern. The new commandment is to love the way He did. Do you want perfect love? Then let Him who displayed perfect love, establish His love in you.

March 17
Read: Deuteronomy 1-2; John 14

John 14:17
"Even the Spirit of truth; whom the world cannot receive, because it seeth him not, neither knoweth him: but ye know him; for he dwelleth with you, and shall be in you."

For the believer, the Bible puts in words what the Spirit teaches in the heart. For the lost, the Bible puts in words what the Spirit convicts in the heart.

March 18
Read: Deuteronomy 3-4; John 15

Deuteronomy 4:20
"But the LORD hath taken you, and brought you forth out of the iron furnace, even out of Egypt, to be unto him a people of inheritance, as ye are this day."

The difference between the Israelites who came out of Egypt and us saints today is that they were brought out of the iron furnace. You and I live in the furnace. *"Beloved, think it not strange concerning the fiery trial which is to try you, as though some strange thing happened unto you"* (I Peter 4:12).

March 19
Read: Deuteronomy 5-6; John 16

Deuteronomy 5:24-27
*"And ye said, Behold, the LORD our God hath shewed us his glory and his greatness, and we have heard his voice out of the midst of the fire: we have seen this day that **God doth talk with man,** and he liveth. ²⁵Now therefore why should we die? for this great fire will consume us: if we hear the voice of the LORD our God any more, then we shall die. ²⁶For who is there of all flesh, that hath heard the voice of the living God speaking out of the midst of the fire, as we have, and lived? ²⁷Go thou near, and hear all that the LORD our God shall say: and speak thou unto us all that the LORD our **God shall speak unto thee; and we will hear it, and do it.**"*

The Israelites had a wonderful privilege of personally hearing from God, but they were overcome with fear and insisted that Moses go and hear from God for them and then tell them what God said. We have men that hear from God today and speak to the church, but too many saints rely on their preacher to tell them what God says instead of going before God and hear for themselves. Heaven has been opened for every true believer, so therefore go and hear what God has to say to you.

March 20
Read: Deuteronomy 7-9; John 17

Deuteronomy 9:24-25
*"Ye have been rebellious against the LORD from the day that I knew you. ²⁵Thus **I fell down before the LORD** forty days and forty nights, **as I fell down at the first**; because the LORD had said he would destroy you."*

We have heard many exhortations on how we can depend on the Lord. But the other side of this can be true as well. God calls people He can depend on. He called Moses because He knew He could depend on Moses to fall on his face every time Israel sinned. Can He depend on you to intercede for others?

March 21
Read: Deuteronomy 10-12; John 18

John 18:28-31
"Then led they Jesus from Caiaphas unto the hall of judgment: and it was early; and they themselves went not into the judgment hall, lest they should be defiled; but that they might eat the passover. ^{29}Pilate then went out unto them, and said, What accusation bring ye against this man? ^{30}They answered and said unto him, If he were not a malefactor, we would not have delivered him up unto thee. ^{31}Then said Pilate unto them, Take ye him, and judge him according to your law. The Jews therefore said unto him, It is not lawful for us to put any man to death."

Those religious leaders sure liked keeping the law. They would dare not break the law while they were delivering Jesus over to be killed. What a contrast, killing Jesus, while keeping the law. This is exactly what false religion is, it is making an outward display while inwardly denying Christ.

March 22
Read: Deuteronomy 13-15; John 19

John 19:5
*"Then came Jesus forth, wearing the crown of thorns, and the purple robe. And Pilate saith unto them, **Behold the man!**"*

If we the church, are ever going to impact our generation, we cannot present Jesus as a man. Although He was fully man as well as fully God, we must demonstrate that He is the Almighty God who saves. BEHOLD THE SON OF GOD!

March 23
Read: Deuteronomy 16-17; John 20-21

John 20:22
"And when he had said this, he breathed on them, and saith unto them, Receive ye the Holy Ghost."

Just as God breathed into Adam's nostrils and he became the first living soul, Jesus breathed on His disciples and they became the first to be born of the Spirit. That very day was the first day that men were BORN AGAIN. From that day on the Spirit of God would dwell in men. 49 days later believers were filled with the Spirit which would usher the born again man out into a dark world and give him the power and boldness to speak against that darkness. Some men want to be filled with the Spirit, but have never been born again; that won't work. Some believers want salvation, but don't want to be filled; they don't work. And last, some believers are filled with the Spirit; they do the work.

March 24
Read: Deuteronomy 18-20; Acts 1

Acts 1:1
*"The former treatise have I made, O Theophilus, of all that Jesus began both to **do** and **teach**..."*

Did you catch the order of these two words "*do and teach*?" Did you notice that "*do*" comes before "*teach*"? Therefore, it is correct to say, "Jesus did not practice what He preached, He preached what He practiced."

March 25
Read: Deuteronomy 21-22; Acts 2

Acts 2:36
*"Therefore let all the house of Israel know assuredly, that **God hath made that same Jesus, whom ye have crucified, both Lord and Christ**."*

If He has been crucified as both Lord and Savior, we can be certain that He was raised as both Lord and Savior. Therefore we have no other choice but to receive Him as both Lord and Savior. He cannot be your Savior without Him being your Lord.

March 26
Read: Deuteronomy 23-24; Acts 3-4

Acts 4:8
"Then Peter, filled with the Holy Ghost, said unto them, Ye rulers of the people, and elders of Israel..."

It is very popular amongst our politicians to use a teleprompter when they speak. Some of them will say some foolish things if they don't have a teleprompter with carefully selected words before them. In my estimation we need some teleprompter preachers. Preachers, who let the Holy Spirit 'tele' them what to say, and allow the Holy Spirit to 'prompt' them when to say it.

March 27
Read: Deuteronomy 25-27; Acts 5

Acts 5:42
"And daily in the temple, and in every house, they ceased not to teach and preach Jesus Christ."

Other Bible translations of this verse say, "preach Jesus **as the** Christ." The point is that the message that the disciples preached was one of proclaiming that Jesus is the Messiah whom they have been waiting for. In America, there are few who have not heard of Jesus. Even the cults and false religions heard of Jesus. We believers in America, no doubt preach that Jesus is the Savior of the world, but we have even a more difficult work before us. We need to preach and demonstrate who the real Jesus is. Preach the real Jesus, not the one made in man's image.

March 28
Read: Deuteronomy 28; Acts 6

Acts 6:3-5
*"Wherefore, brethren, look ye out among you seven men of honest report, **full of the Holy Ghost** and wisdom, whom we may appoint over this business. ⁴But we will give ourselves continually to prayer,*

*and to the ministry of the word. ⁵And the saying pleased the whole multitude: and they chose **Stephen, a man full of faith and of the Holy Ghost**, and Philip, and Prochorus, and Nicanor, and Timon, and Parmenas, and Nicolas a proselyte of Antioch."*

This world has seen few men the caliber of Stephen. Stephen was selected with the other Spirit filled men and it was noted that He was full of the Spirit. It is one thing to be filled; it is another for it to be obvious to the onlookers. The world cannot tolerate men like Stephen; he was so full of God that the world quickly killed him off. However, Stephen left something behind. It was a prayer; I believe one of the most powerful prayers ever prayed. *"Lord, lay not this sin to their charge."* The great apostle Paul was there that day, and I don't have to tell you the effects he had on this world. We still read what he penned today. Hallelujah, we need some Spirit filled men after the order of Stephen.

March 29
Read: Deuteronomy 29-30; Acts 7

Deuteronomy 29:29
"The secret things belong unto the LORD our God: but those things which are revealed belong unto us and to our children for ever, that we may do all the words of this law."

We must never force revelation knowledge. Those secret things belong to God and He alone will share His secrets as He sees fit. A lot of false doctrine comes from those who want to know God's secrets before He finds them fit to be responsible with the revelation He gives them. I don't know about you, but I am glad God has some secrets. Secrets are shared amongst those of the most intimate relationships. The more I know Him the more He shares His secrets.

March 30
Read: Deuteronomy 31; Acts 8

Deuteronomy 31:25-26
"That Moses commanded the Levites, which bare the ark of the covenant of the LORD, saying, ²⁶Take this book of the law, and put it in the side of the ark of the covenant of the LORD your God, that it may be there for a witness against thee."

The book of the law, which is the word of God, was put next to the ark as a witness against Israel. Today, the living word of God Jesus, is next to the Father, but He is there not as a witness against us but as an intercessor for us. HALLELUJAH!

March 31
Read: Deuteronomy 32; Acts 9

Acts 9:22
"But Saul increased the more in strength, and confounded the Jews which dwelt at Damascus, proving that this is very Christ."

At this present time in Saul's life, the only Bible he had was the Old Testament. But this testament was not old for Him. On the road to Damascus, he had a revelation of Christ and Christ made that Old Testament brand new. I don't know about you but I sure love reading my NEW Old Testament.

April

April 1
Read: Deuteronomy 33-34; Acts 10

Deuteronomy 34:10
*"And Moses went up from the plains of Moab **unto the mountain of Nebo, to the top of Pisgah,** that is over against Jericho. And the LORD shewed him all the land of Gilead, unto Dan."*

Moses climbed Mount Sinai to receive the law; he also climbed it to see God through the cleft of a rock. Now he climbed another mountain, *"To the top of Pisgah"* to view the Promised Land. It was there that he died. Moses shows up again some centuries later. *"And after six days Jesus taketh Peter, James, and John his brother, and bringeth them **up into an high mountain** apart, ²And was transfigured before them: and his face did shine as the sun, and his raiment was white as the light. ³And, behold, **there appeared unto them** Moses and Elias talking with him"* (Matthew 17:1-3). It seems you just can't keep a mountain climber down. We need some mountain climbers in the church today. Men and woman who desire that higher plain with God. Psalm 78:35 says, *"And they remembered that God was their rock, and the **high God** their redeemer."* He is a high God, and if you want to walk with Him and know Him intimately, you must leave this lower life behind and start climbing and never come down.

April 2
Read: Joshua 1-3; Acts 11-12

Acts 11:21-23
*"And the hand of the Lord was with them: and a great number believed, and turned unto the Lord. ²²Then tidings of these things came unto the ears of the church which was in Jerusalem: and they sent forth Barnabas, that he should go as far as Antioch. ²³Who, when he came, and **had seen the grace of God**, was glad, and exhorted them all, that with purpose of heart they would cleave unto the Lord."*

Barnabas, while in Jerusalem, heard that a great number of people turned unto the Lord. So the elders sent forth Barnabas, so he could exhort them to cleave to the Lord. The first thing he did when he arrived in that region was to see the grace of God. That means that he saw in the believers a genuine conversion to the truth. Saint, it is not judgmental after all for you to expect to see the life of Christ in someone after you heard they turned to Christ.

Extra:
Acts 12:1
"Now about that time Herod the king stretched forth his hands to vex certain of the church."

The believers in Christ did not need Herod's permission to be the church. Neither do we need anyone's permission.

April 3
Read: Joshua 4-5; Acts 13

Acts 13:11-12
"And now, behold, the hand of the Lord is upon thee, and thou shalt be blind, not seeing the sun for a season. And immediately there fell on him a mist and a darkness; and he went about seeking some to lead him by the hand. ¹²Then the deputy, when he saw what was done, believed, **being astonished at the doctrine of the Lord***."*

It is one thing to teach, or make known to others, the doctrine of the Lord. It is another thing when you can teach or preach it with such power that others will be astonished with the doctrine.

April 4
Read: Joshua 6-7; Acts 14

Joshua 6:10
"And Joshua had commanded the people, saying, Ye shall not shout, nor make any noise with your voice, neither shall any word proceed out of your mouth, until the day I bid you shout; then shall ye shout."

God through Joshua told Israel to march around those walls of Jericho and to not make a peep. No back talking, no spreading doubt and fear, no infecting people with unbelief. Just keep your mouth shut and obey God.

April 5
Read: Joshua 8-9; Acts 15

Joshua 8:34-35
"And afterward he read all the words of the law, the blessings and cursings, according to all that is written in the book of the law. ^{35}There was not a word of all that Moses commanded, which Joshua read not before **all the congregation of Israel, with the women, and the little ones, and the strangers** *that were conversant among them."*

We shouldn't be so quick, as is such a common thing today, to divide up the body of Christ into different age groups and different lifestyle groups. The reading and the preaching of the word of God can and should be to the whole congregation of the Lord, *"with the women and the CHILDREN."*

April 6
Read: Joshua 10-11; Acts 16

Joshua 10:6
"And the men of Gibeon sent unto Joshua to the camp to Gilgal, saying, Slack not thy hand from thy servants; come up to us quickly, **and save us, and help us***: for all the kings of the Amorites that dwell in the mountains are gathered together against us."*

How refreshing to read about the world asking the church for help instead of the church asking the world for help.

April 7
Read: Joshua 12-14; Acts 17-18

Acts 17:10-11
"And the brethren immediately sent away Paul and Silas by night unto Berea: who coming thither went into the synagogue of the Jews. ¹¹These were more noble than those in Thessalonica, in that they received the word with all readiness of mind, and searched the scriptures daily, whether those things were so."

Too often the saints settle for the idea that every church is going to have things that are wrong and have people who refuse to be faithful to the word of God. I guess that brings some kind of comfort to the people to think that they are not expected to, as a church, walk in a manner that fully pleases God and really demonstrate a true New Testament church. However, if a town called Berea can have people, who were not yet born again believers, be committed to search the scriptures, why would we think that we cannot be a part of a church that has most, if not all the members committed with a readiness of mind and search out the scriptures daily to live by them?

April 8
Read: Joshua 15-16; Acts 19

Acts 19:2
"He said unto them, Have ye received the Holy Ghost since ye believed?"

By Paul's question, we can see that this Christian life is much more than just being "saved." God didn't just save us to take us to heaven; He saved us so He could fill us with Himself. Saint, let it sink in. You have the highest privilege in all of this vast universe. This great God wants to live in you. He wants to fill you with nothing but Himself. Will you let Him?

April 9
Read: Joshua 17-18; Acts 20

Acts 20:26-27
"Wherefore I take you to record this day, that I am pure from the blood of all men. ²⁷For I have not shunned to declare unto you all the counsel of God."

Paul was pure from the blood of all men. The main reason is that he preached the whole counsel of God. The seeker sensitive preachers of our day, who preach what the people want to hear, are not able to say that they are pure from the blood of men. To bring this to a more personal level, do you believe and live the whole counsel of God? Do you believe the whole Bible? Do you believe it is all for today? You may believe 99 percent of it is for today, but that is not the WHOLE counsel. The whole counsel makes whole.

April 10
Read: Joshua 19-20; Acts 21

Acts 21:13-14
*"Then Paul answered, What mean ye to weep and to break mine heart? for I am ready not to be bound only, but also to die at Jerusalem for the name of the Lord Jesus. ¹⁴And when he would not be **persuaded**, we ceased, saying, The will of the Lord be done."*

When just one believer is persuaded to do the Lord's will, it can result in others conceding to let *"the will of the Lord be done."*

April 11
Read: Joshua 21-22; Acts 22

Acts 22:18
"And saw him saying unto me, Make haste, and get thee quickly out of Jerusalem: for they will not receive thy testimony concerning me."

We all know that the Lord allows us to go through many trials to perfect us, but don't forget that sometimes He leads us totally out of and away from problems too.

April 12
Read: Joshua 23-24; Acts 23

Joshua 23:6
"Be ye therefore very courageous to keep and to do all that is written in the book of the law of Moses, that ye turn not aside therefrom to the right hand or to the left."

Israel for the most part had conquered Canaan Land. Now Israel was at rest and it was a right time to set up their government. So Joshua said *"Be ye therefore very courageous to keep and to do all that is written in the book...."* That book of the Law of Moses was all the law and order they needed. We have the Law of Moses plus more. We have an Old and New Testament. If the Law of Moses was sufficient to govern Israel, then our Bibles are more than sufficient to govern us. So our governing authority today is, *"Be ye therefore very courageous to keep and to do all that is written in the book...."*

April 13
Read: Judges 1-2; Acts 24-25

Acts 24:25, 26:24,28
"Now as he reasoned about righteousness, self-control, and the judgment to come, Felix was afraid and answered, "Go away for now; when I have a convenient time I will call for you -
^{24}Now as he thus made his defense, Festus said with a loud voice, "Paul, you are beside yourself! Much learning is driving you mad! -
^{28}Then Agrippa said to Paul, "You almost persuade me to become a Christian."

Paul testified before two governors and one king. He got a reaction out of all three. Felix got scared, Festus told Paul he was a mad man and King Agrippa was almost persuaded to be a Christian. The scriptures do not tell us if any of these men were persuaded to the point that they became a Christian, but one thing is clear, Paul preached with authority and power. We believers don't save souls, we preach to them. We must preach to get a reaction. Not by irritating people so they finally shout back in anger, but with genuine Holy Ghost authority. You cannot do this unless you are filled with the Spirit. We don't need evangelism techniques and outreaches; we need believers to be filled with the Spirit.

April 14
Read: Judges 3-4; Acts 26

Acts 26:15-18
*"And I said, Who art thou, Lord? And he said, I am Jesus whom thou persecutest. ¹⁶But rise, and stand upon thy feet: for I have appeared unto thee for this purpose, to make thee a minister and a witness both of these things which thou hast seen, and of those things in the which I will appear unto thee; ¹⁷Delivering thee from the people, and from the Gentiles, unto whom now I send thee, ¹⁸**To open their eyes, and to turn them from darkness to light, and from the power of Satan unto God**, that they may receive forgiveness of sins, and inheritance among them which are sanctified by faith that is in me."*

Our evangelism would take on such a different tone and be more impactful if we would understand that true salvation is more than just a person turning from a bad life to a good one. It is more than just adding Jesus to their life. True salvation brings a person out from under the power of Satan. It is more than just a person saying some simple prayer and then they go on their merry way without any real sense of freedom entering their soul. When a person really gets saved, they are delivered from the power of Satan. Our evangelism must be bold, it must make hell tremble and it must break the power of darkness.

April 15
Read: Judges 5-6; Acts 27

Judges 6:25-26
"And it came to pass the same night, that the LORD said unto him, Take thy father's young bullock, even the second bullock of seven years old, **and throw down the altar of Baal that thy father hath, and cut down the grove that is by it:** *²⁶And build an altar unto the LORD thy God upon the top of this rock, in the ordered place, and take the second bullock, and offer a burnt sacrifice with the wood of the grove which thou shalt cut down."*

Just because dad may serve Baal, or as far as that goes, mom, brother, sister, or aunt and uncle serves Baal, it does not mean that you have to. God demanded for Gideon to tear down that altar to a false God, even if it was his own father's, and God still demands it today. It is God we must all answer too; so resist any influence from family and friends who encourages you to seek out something else. Love the Lord your God with all your heart, soul, mind and strength.

April 16
Read: Judges 7-8; Acts 28 – Romans 1

Judges 7:19-20
"So Gideon, and the hundred men that were with him, came unto the outside of the camp in the beginning of the middle watch; and they had but newly set the watch: and they blew the trumpets, and brake the pitchers that were in their hands. ²⁰And the three companies blew the trumpets, and **brake the pitchers, and held the lamps in their left hands,** *and the trumpets in their right hands to blow withal: and they cried, The sword of the LORD, and of Gideon."*

The only way Gideon and his boys were going to let the light from those lamps be seen was by breaking the pitchers that were holding them. The only way this world is going to see the fire of God shining from us is if we allow ourselves to be broken.

April 17
Read: Judges 9-10; Romans 2-3

Romans 2:16
"In the day when God shall judge the secrets of men by Jesus Christ according to my gospel."

If you don't have any secrets, there won't be anything to judge. Keep your heart exposed before God.

April 18
Read: Judges 11-12; Romans 4-5

Romans 5:20
*"Moreover the law entered, that the offence might abound. But where sin abounded, **grace did much more abound**."*

Sin is an action of man; grace is the greater reaction of God. So much for the law of physics that says, "For every action there is an opposite and equal reaction."

April 19
Read: Judges 13-14; Romans 6- 7

Romans 6:11
*"Likewise **reckon** ye also yourselves to be dead indeed unto sin, but alive unto God through Jesus Christ our Lord."*

Paul said, *"I am crucified with Christ:"* That applies to us as well. If my flesh is crucified with Christ then why do I feel like it is so alive? That is because I must reckon myself to be dead. Too reckon myself dead means two things, first it means that I am not really dead, second it means that I must play dead. When I was a young boy I used to play army with the other neighborhood boys. If I came running around a garage and one of the other boys was there he would start shooting me with his make believe machine gun. Of course, when he had a machine gun he couldn't miss. So he got me. I then had to act like I really got shot and do some dramatic flip or roll as I hit the ground to try to make it look as if I really got killed. Whenever one of us really did a good job acting out our death the other would say, "good die." Saint, reckon yourself dead. Do such a good job that someone will come up to you and say, "good die."

April 20
Read: Judges 15-16; Romans 8

Judges 15:18
*"And he was sore athirst, **and called on the LORD, and said,** Thou hast given this great deliverance into the hand of thy servant: and now shall I die for thirst, and fall into the hand of the uncircumcised?"*

This is the first time it is recorded that Samson ever called upon the Lord. He did one more time at the end of his life. That was the problem with Samson, he was a walking witness of the power of God, but he never seemed to give any glory to God for it. When he finally did call upon the name of the Lord, he recognized that God did deliver him but he quickly followed it up with a complaint; *"and now shall I die for thirst, and fall into the hand of the uncircumcised?"* Since that was the extent of Samson's calling upon the Lord, he did tragically fall into the hands of the uncircumcised. Let this be a lesson to us all to give glory to God for all His blessings in our life. Let's thank Him daily, not fill our prayers with complaints.

April 21
Read: Judges 17-18; Romans 9-10

Romans 10:9,13
*"That if thou shalt confess with thy mouth the **Lord** Jesus, and shalt believe in thine heart that God hath raised him from the dead, thou shalt be saved....¹³For whosoever shall call upon the name of the **Lord** shall be saved."*

Some of our modern evangelist preach Jesus as our Savior. There is no disputing that fact, but they have failed to preach Him as Lord. Verse nine says to confess the **Lord** Jesus; verse thirteen says call upon the name of the **Lord**. Simply put, Jesus is the Lord that came to save us. He saved us to be our Lord. You can't have Jesus the Savior without Him being your Lord. We need to preach the LORD JESUS will save.

April 22
Read: Judges 19; Romans 11-12

Romans 12:9
*"**Let love** be without dissimulation. Abhor that which is evil; cleave to that which is good."*

The word *"let"* was added by the translators to accentuate the nature of agape love. You don't make love work and you don't force love, you let love work. We would not have such a hard time loving, if we would let God, who is love, love through us. The last thing you will ever have to do is try to get God to love. It is His nature to love. The God in you wants to love others through you. Will you let Him?

April 23
Read: Judges 20-21; Romans 13-14

Romans 14:17
*"For the kingdom of God is not meat and drink; but righteousness, and peace, and **joy in the Holy Ghost.**"*

When I was a young boy in the Catholic Church, I used to think the more somber a person was the more holy they were. The less the priest showed any kind of emotion the holier he was. Isn't that totally contrary to what the kingdom of God is? It is joy in the Holy Ghost!

April 24
Read: Ruth 1-2; Romans 15-16

Ruth 1:1,6
"Now it came to pass in the days when the judges ruled, that there was a famine in the land. And a certain man of Bethlehemjudah went to sojourn in the country of Moab, he, and his wife, and his two sons... ⁶Then she arose with her daughters in law, that she might return from the country of Moab: for she had heard in the country of Moab how that the LORD had visited his people in giving them bread."

God uses people's difficulties and troubles to fulfill His will. This famine was not by accident. This was God's way to get the godly Ruth out of the land of Moab and bring her to Israel to be in the lineage of the Savior of the world, Jesus Christ.

April 25
Read: Ruth 3-4; I Corinthians 1-2

I Corinthians 2:16
"For who hath known the mind of the Lord, that he may instruct him? But we have the mind of Christ."

The less you have of the mind of Christ the more attractive your own ideas become.

April 26
Read: I Samuel 1-2; I Corinthians 3-4

I Corinthians 3:11-13
*"For other foundation can no man lay than that is laid, which is Jesus Christ. ¹²Now if any man build upon this foundation gold, silver, precious stones, **wood, hay, stubble**; ¹³Every man's work shall be made manifest: for the day shall declare it, because it shall be revealed by fire; and the fire shall try every man's work of what sort it is."*

The reason some churches and ministries, that are nothing more than man's agenda, seem so huge and successful is because the cheaper the building materials, the bigger you can build.

April 27
Read: I Samuel 3-5; I Corinthians 5-6

I Samuel 3:1-4
"And the child Samuel ministered unto the LORD before Eli. And the word of the LORD was precious in those days; there was no open vision. ²And it came to pass at that time, when Eli was laid down in his place, and his eyes began to wax dim, that he could not see; ³And ere the lamp of God went out in the temple of the LORD, where the ark of God was, and Samuel was laid down to sleep; **⁴That the LORD called Samuel: and he answered, Here am I.**"

Even when it seems there is no desire for God anywhere; even if it seems all of society has turned from God; even when it seems that the lamp of God has grown dim and gone out in much of the church today; God will still call the names of those who will listen and obey His voice. God still has a people for Himself. Are you one of them?

April 28
Read: I Samuel 6-8; I Corinthians 7

I Samuel 8:7
"And the LORD said unto Samuel, Hearken unto the voice of the people in all that they say unto thee: for ***they have not rejected thee, but they have rejected me****, that I should not reign over them."*

Whenever you stand unwavering for the truth you will face rejection. The rejection that will be the hardest to deal with is when that rejection comes from those who consider themselves Christians. It is hard to face rejection when it comes from your brethren. It can lead to hurt feelings that can fester into bitterness. However, if you always remember that when other believers reject you for holding to the truth, they are not rejecting you, but God; this will help you get a burden for your brethren and go before the Lord in prayer for them.

April 29
Read: I Samuel 9-11; I Corinthians 8-9

I Corinthians 8:2-3
"And if any man think that he knoweth any thing, he knoweth nothing yet as he ought to know. ³But if any man love God, the same is known of him."

The real men and women of God are recognized, not so much by what they know about God, but by their love for God.

April 30
Read: I Samuel 12-13; I Corinthians 10

I Corinthians 10:18-19
*"For first of all, when ye come together in the church, I hear that there be divisions among you; and I partly believe it. ¹⁹**For there must be also heresies among you**, that they which are approved may be made manifest among you."*

We all hate that there is division in the body of Christ. It is one of the worst testimonies to this world the church has. Yet, there is a positive side about division. Paul stated that division in the body of Christ will reveal those who are approved, those who are the true believers. Real division will separate the sheep from the goats, the wheat from the tares and the true from the false. Though I hate all the seeker sensitive techniques and mega church mentality that has overcome the church, God can still use it for good. God has allowed the seeker sensitive and mega churches to attract all the goats, tares and uncommitted so they do not come and stir up trouble in the Spirit led and Spirit filled body of Christ.

May

May 1
Read: I Samuel 14; I Corinthians 11

I Samuel 14:24
*"And the men of Israel were distressed that day, for **Saul had placed the people under oath**, saying, "Cursed is the man who eats any food until evening, before I have taken vengeance on my enemies." So none of the people tasted food."*

In chapter 13 we learned that Saul's kingdom would not continue because he did a foolish thing. Many times it happens when Christians lose their anointing from God, they gravitate toward extreme religious rules. At the least appropriate time, Saul did that and called for a fast. It is apparent that he was not led of the Lord to do this. He attempted to compensate for losing God's favor by impressing others with a false spiritual fervor. As he *"placed the people under oath,"* all he did was put the people in distress. Let it be that your commitment to God promotes in others a liberty and greater desire for God, not cause distress.

May 2
Read: I Samuel 15-16; I Corinthians 12-13

I Samuel 16:6-7
*"And it came to pass, when they were come, that he looked on Eliab, and said, **Surely the LORD'S anointed is before him**. ⁷But the LORD said unto Samuel, Look not on his countenance, or on the height of his stature; because I have refused him: for the LORD seeth not as man seeth; for man looketh on the outward appearance, but the LORD looketh on the heart."*

Some Christians have eluded to this scripture when they are trying to hide or justify their less than Christian behavior. They say in response to those who challenge them, "You are looking at the outward, but God knows my heart." I don't know if Christians really grasp the truth of what they are saying. That should cause every Christian to tremble, to know that God does know their heart. Man can be fooled, but God isn't. He also knows the heart of every Christian when they are raising their hands in worship at church.

May 3
Read: I Samuel 17; I Corinthians 14

I Samuel 17:2-4, 24, 51-52
"And Saul and the men of Israel were gathered together, and pitched by the valley of Elah, and set the battle in array against the Philistines. ³And the Philistines stood on a mountain on the one side, and Israel stood on a mountain on the other side: and there was a valley between them. ⁴And there went out a champion out of the camp of the Philistines, named Goliath, of Gath, whose height was six cubits and a span....²⁴And all the men of Israel, when they saw the man, fled from him, and were sore afraid....⁵¹Therefore David ran, and stood upon the Philistine, and took his sword, and drew it out of the sheath thereof, and slew him, and cut off his head therewith. And when the Philistines saw their champion was dead, they fled. ⁵²And the men of Israel and of Judah arose, and shouted, and pursued the Philistines, until thou come to the valley, and to the gates of Ekron. And the wounded of the Philistines fell down by the way to Shaaraim, even unto Gath, and unto Ekron."

The men who feared the giant when Saul was leading were the same men who pursued the Philistines when David led the charge. It really does matter what kind of leadership you have over you.

May 4
Read: I Samuel 18-19; I Corinthians 15

I Corinthians 15:17
"And if Christ be not raised, your faith is vain; ye are yet in your sins."

It is true that Jesus nailed our sins to the cross. It is true that we find redemption through His blood. But the cross and the blood alone are not sufficient. There is one more thing of the utmost importance, THE RESURRECTION. The scriptures are clear, if Christ was not raised, then we are all still in our sins. In the blood of Christ we find forgiveness for our sin, but it is in the resurrection that we have victory over our sin. Hallelujah!

May 5
Read: I Samuel 20-21; I Corinthians 16 – II Corinthians 1

I Corinthians 16:9
"For a great door and effectual is opened unto me, and there are many adversaries."

Many adversaries go along with every effectual ministry.

May 6
Read: I Samuel 22-23; II Corinthians 2-4

I Samuel 23:16
"And Jonathan Saul's son arose, and went to David into the wood, and strengthened his hand in God."

Jonathon had previously confessed that he knew one day that David would be king. Instead of being jealous over David, Jonathon loved and supported David, even when his father Saul was hunting him down. Jonathon's life was cut short because of his backslidden father's poor leadership, but there is one great thing that he did before he was killed in battle. He went to David who was hiding out in the wilderness and encouraged him. He *"strengthened his hand in God."* David did go on to be king. Jonathon's encouragement lived on in David. I want to be an encourager, how about you?

May 7
Read: I Samuel 24-25; II Corinthians 5-6

II Corinthians 6:17
*"Wherefore come out from among them, **and be ye separate**, saith the Lord, and touch not the unclean thing; and I will receive you."*

Just as God has said, let not man separate what He has joined together, so too, let not men join together what God has separated.

May 8
Read: I Samuel 26-27; II Corinthians 7-8

II Corinthians 7:3
"I speak not this to condemn you: for I have said before, that ye are in our hearts to die and live with you."

Paul had a love for the church that our generation does not seem to comprehend. Yet, we could have that love too if we would love Christ as we should. The more we would love Christ, the more we would see that the church is Christ's body. Tell me if you can, have you ever loved anyone just for their head?

May 9
Read: I Samuel 28-29; II Corinthians 9-10

II Corinthians 9:8
*"And God is able to make all grace abound toward you; that ye, always having all sufficiency in all things, **may abound to every good work**."*

Christ is sufficient for all things. He meets the needs. Maybe the lack of funds and the lack of workers and just the general struggle so many ministries go through to stay afloat, could be because they might be doing a work, but they might not being doing God's good work. Hudson Taylor the great missionary to China said, "God's work done in God's way will never lack God's supply." The challenge is not to find the resources; the challenge is to know the will and work of God.

May 10
Read: I Samuel 30-31; II Corinthians 11

II Corinthians 11:2
"For I am jealous over you with godly jealousy: for I have espoused you to one husband, that I may present you as a chaste virgin to Christ."

There is a desperate call today for the church to come together in unity. However, true unity will never happen until ministers espouse the flock of God to the ONE husband, the Lord Christ Jesus.

May 11
Read: II Samuel 1-2; II Corinthians 12-13

II Corinthians 12:5-7
*"Of such an one will I glory: yet of myself I will not glory, but in mine infirmities. ⁶For though I would desire to glory, I shall not be a fool; for I will say the truth: but now I forbear, lest any man should think of me above that which he seeth me to be, or that he heareth of me. ⁷And lest I should be **exalted above measure through the abundance of the revelations**, there was given to me a thorn in the flesh, the messenger of Satan to buffet me, lest I should be exalted above measure."*

Paul in his first letter to the Corinthians taught that knowledge puffs up. Here in II Corinthians, he makes it clear that an abundance of revelations can also cause one to become proud. There is no one who knows this better than me. I have repented, and do repent for considering other Christians less spiritual than me because they don't get some things that the Lord has showed me. Revelation comes from God, not from our self. Love revelation knowledge and seek God for more, but beware that you too can get proud.

May 12
Read: II Samuel 3-5; Galatians 1-2

Galatians 1:12
"*For I neither received it of man, neither was I taught it, but by the **revelation** of Jesus Christ.*"

Discipline without revelation is mere religion.

May 13
Read: II Samuel 6-8; Galatians 3-4

II Samuel 7:18
"*Then went king David in, and sat before the LORD, and he said, Who am I, O Lord GOD? and what is my house, that **thou hast brought me hitherto**?*"

Every faithful Christian who has followed after the Lord for many years has faced numerous trials, tribulations and temptations. No doubt they went through dark valleys and crossed dry and weary lands. Yet those who have remained faithful don't pat themselves on the back and say, "What a strong believer I am." Even though they have been determined to follow the Lord they can't help but to say, "*Who am I, O Lord*, that you have brought me this far."

May 14
Read: II Samuel 9-11; Galatians 5-6

Galatians 5:16-18
"*This I say then, Walk in the Spirit, and ye shall not fulfil the lust of the flesh. ¹⁷For the flesh lusteth against the Spirit, and the Spirit against the flesh: and these are contrary the one to the other: so that ye cannot do the things that ye would. ¹⁸But if ye be led of the Spirit, ye are not under the law.*"

Paul didn't say to them, if you don't fulfill the lust of the flesh you will walk in the Spirit, he said, "*Walk in the Spirit, and ye shall not fulfil the lust of the flesh.*" Saints, this is how you walk in victory over the flesh.

May 15
Read: II Samuel 12-13; Ephesians 1-2

Ephesians 1:1
*"Paul, an apostle of Jesus Christ by the will of God, to the saints which are at Ephesus, and **to the faithful** in Christ Jesus."*

Paul's letter to the Ephesians was to the saints and the faithful. Yes, there are saints that remain faithful, no matter what life and the devil throw at them. There are some that waver at times, and some who backslide for a season. If you are one of the faithful, and you sometimes wonder if you are doing anything for the kingdom of God, let me assure you that you are. While other Christians may go back to the world to look for something they think they are missing, they are still seeing you be faithful. You who are faithful are holding down the fort, so to speak, while others drift. When they come back, they have a special appreciation for those who have remained faithful. Today, if you haven't been, you can start a life of faithfulness.

May 16
Read: II Samuel 14-15; Ephesians 3-4

Ephesians 3:19
*"And to know the **love of Christ, which passeth knowledge**, that ye might be filled with all the fulness of God."*

Knowledge can be obtained through the many Christian resources there are today. You can get knowledge through spending money to go to Bible college. However, love that surpasses knowledge is gained by pursuing Christ.

May 17
Read: II Samuel 16-17; Ephesians 5-6

Ephesians 5:27
*"That he might present it to himself a glorious church, not having **spot**, or wrinkle, or any such thing; but that it should be holy and without blemish."*

If you went for an x-ray on your lungs and found out you had a spot on them, would you just shrug it off or would you have enough concern to find out what it is and see if you need to get it removed? I believe none of us reading this would be happy with that spot. I am talking about the physical body, but what about the spiritual body? Should we not all the more want to see the spots of worldliness and sin that keeps us unclean before the Lord removed? Repentance is the best spot remover ever.

May 18
Read: II Samuel 18; Philippians 1

Philippians 1:12
"But I would ye should understand, brethren, that the things which happened unto me have fallen out rather unto the furtherance of the gospel."

What a comfort to know that whatever the trial, temptation and difficulty may be, God makes all things work together for our own personal good. It is even a greater comfort to know, that when things happen to us, the gospel can actually be advanced. Let what must come, come, and let the gospel go forward.

May 19
Read: II Samuel 19-20; Philippians 2

II Samuel 19:10
*"And Absalom, **whom we anointed** over us, is dead in battle. Now therefore why speak ye not a word of bringing the king back?"*

Absalom was the people's choice, David was God's choice. Absalom had the people's favor, David had God's anointing. Whatever you have chosen and anointed over yourself other than Jesus as king, must die. Bring back the anointed King. We need God's anointed, not the people's anointed. The people's anointed just ends in death.

May 20
Read: II Samuel 21-22; Philippians 3-4

Philippians 3:17
"Brethren, be followers together of me, and mark them which walk so as ye have us for an ensample."

No matter how much we hear the words, "Who are you to judge," everyone will judge. It is just about impossible to not judge. The church is even told that they are to righteously judge the church. So what I am getting to is, you will be judged, you will be marked, one way or another. Romans 16:17 says to, *"mark them which cause divisions and offenses."* So, how will you be marked? Will you have the mark of good example, or will you have the mark of division and offenses? There is no way out of this, people are watching.

May 21
Read: II Samuel 23-24; Colossians 1-2

Colossians 2:6
"As ye have therefore received Christ Jesus the Lord, so walk ye in him."

I am sure it has happened to all of us where someone comes along and complicates Christianity. They get you all confused by presenting to you their ideas, interpretations and self-convictions. When this happens you need to clear your mind of these things and just go back and walk in the simple faith and obedience that you received when you first got saved. That never expires, you never outgrow that.

May 22
Read: I Kings 1; Colossians 3-4

Colossians 3:2
*"**Set** your **affection** on things above, not on things on the earth."*

Notice that it says "affection," (singular) not affections (plural). There can be a wide variety of things that people can have affections for, but there is only one important affection, it is Christ. He must be our whole desire; He must be our all in all. When you pour concrete into a form and it hardens, it is said to be **set**. You cannot change the shape of it any more. Likewise, let your heart be set on Him.

May 23
Read: I Kings 2; I Thessalonians 1-2

I Kings 2:11-12
*"And the days that David reigned over Israel were forty years: seven years reigned he in Hebron, and thirty and three years reigned he in Jerusalem. ¹²**Then sat Solomon upon the throne** of David his father; and his kingdom was established greatly."*

David did not get much of a chance to sit on his throne. For much of his life he was on the run. Ten times in I Samuel there is reference to David having to escape. David *"avoided; slipped away; down through a window; fled and escaped; fled; hid himself; fled; departed and escaped; escaped; made haste to get away;"* That is the cost to be a man after God's own heart (Acts 13:22). His wife despised him, King Saul tried to kill him and even his own son Absalom wanted him dead. Jesus did say, *"And a man's foes shall be they of his own household"* (Matthew 10:36). On the other hand, we have King Solomon basking in the reputation of his father David. Solomon started out by plopping himself down on the throne. Solomon went on to anger the Lord for he married foreign wives. One of them was even the daughter of Pharaoh. Beware Christian of that life of ease; beware of that place of importance over men. If you plop yourself down on the throne, you are surely headed for disaster.

May 24
Read: I Kings 3-4; I Thessalonians 3-4

I Thessalonians 4:16
***"For the Lord himself shall descend from heaven with a shout**, with the voice of the archangel, and with the trump of God: and the dead in Christ shall rise first."*

Our Lord has been waiting two thousand years for that day He can shout; what a shout it will be!

May 25
Read: I Kings 5-6; I Thessalonians 5 - II Thessalonians 1

I Kings 6:7
"And the house, when it was in building, was built of stone made ready before it was brought thither: so that there was neither hammer nor axe nor any tool of iron heard in the house, while it was in building."

Peter said, *"Ye also, **as lively stones**, are built up a spiritual house, an holy priesthood, to offer up spiritual sacrifices, acceptable to God by Jesus Christ"* (I Peter 2:5). Tares, wolves and the unconverted are not suitable building material for the house of God. Only lively stones will be used to build the spiritual house.

May 26

Read: I Kings 7; II Thessalonians 2-3

II Thessalonians 3:14
"And if any man obey not our word by this epistle, note that man, and have no company with him, that he may be ashamed."

If this verse was practiced with real spiritual discernment, some churches would get pretty empty.

May 27
Read: I Kings 8; I Timothy 1-2

I Kings 8:26
"And now, O God of Israel, let thy word, ***I pray thee****, be verified, which thou spakest unto thy servant David my father."*

Chapter eight of I Kings has more reference to prayer than any other chapter in the Bible. The words, "pray, prayer, prayeth, praying" and "supplication" are found a total of twenty five times. It starts at verse twenty six and goes on to verse fifty nine. For the remainder of the chapter, sacrifices are offered up to God. It is only appropriate that this chapter is so much about prayer because Solomon is dedicating the temple unto the Lord. Prayer goes along with dedication. What would make any Christian think they can dedicate their life to God without prayer being very instrumental in that dedication? Would God receive our offering of a living sacrifice without it being made ready through prayer? There seems to be very little dedication today; it can only be that there is very little prayer.

May 28
Read: I Kings 9-10; I Timothy 3-4

I Kings 10:1
"And when the queen of Sheba heard of the ***fame of Solomon concerning the name of the LORD****, she came to prove him with hard questions."*

Some Christians have made a name for themselves; some have made a name for the Lord. Who does your life reveal?

May 29
Read: I Kings 11; I Timothy 5-6

I Timothy 6:20
"O Timothy, keep that which is committed to thy trust, ***avoiding profane and vain babblings****, and oppositions of science falsely so called."*

You must avoid vain babblings. What is vain babbling? It means empty sounding, fruitless discussion. What causes empty discussion? It comes from empty people; people who are void of the Holy Spirit. It comes from saints who do not walk after the Spirit. If you will take serious the mandate to be filled with the Spirit, you will never babble on with empty words, nor will you give an ear to babblers. It is one thing to talk and argue, it is another to speak by the Spirit of truth.

May 30
Read: I Kings 12-13; II Timothy 1-2

I Kings 12:31-32
"And he made an house of high places, and made priests of the lowest of the people, which were not of the sons of Levi. ³²And Jeroboam ordained a feast in the eighth month, on the fifteenth day of the month, **like unto the feast that is in Judah***, and he offered upon the altar. So did he in Bethel, sacrificing unto the calves that he had made: and he placed in Bethel the priests of the high places which he had made."*

Jeroboam, to some degree, mimicked the worship that was carried out in the house of the Lord in Jerusalem, by building a house of high places and ordaining a feast, "like unto the feast that is in Judah." However, it was a fraud. Today we have something similar. It happens on Sunday mornings at the same time that true believers come together in unity and worship in Spirit and truth. We have those who call themselves the church, who meet on Sunday mornings as well, except one main thing is missing, the presence of the Lord. Without the Lord's presence, it is no church. Saint of God, are you in the presence of the Lord where you gather for worship?

May 31
Read: I Kings 14-15; II Timothy 3-4

II Timothy 4:4
"And they shall turn away their ears from the truth, **and shall be turned unto fables.***"*

The greatest fable of all is telling the story of another or different Christ.

June

June 1
Read: I Kings 16-17; Titus 1-3

Titus 2:9-10
*"Exhort servants to be obedient unto their own masters, and to please them well in all things; not answering again; ¹⁰Not purloining, but shewing all good fidelity; that they **may adorn the doctrine of God** our Saviour in all things."*

Paul in writing to Titus, exhorts servants to obey their masters. He further says that when they do this, they are adding to biblical doctrine by adorning it. They are not adding words, which we are forbidden to do, but they are dressing it up and making it more attractive. Just like when you wrap a present in paper and bows and ribbons, it makes the present more exciting and attractive. On the other hand, when we are disobedient to the word we malign it. We take away from the beauty of it. No wonder some people hate the word of God and they never even read it. They have seen a bad version of it in some people who claim to live it.

June 2
Read: I Kings 18-19; Philemon - Hebrews 1

I Kings 18:21
*"And Elijah came unto all the people, and said, How long halt ye between two opinions? if the LORD be God, follow him: but if Baal, then follow him. **And the people answered him not a word.**"*

The people answered *"not a word"* because there was not much evidence in the life of the people of what god they should serve. Once Elijah called down the fire, there was no longer a doubt. Saints, we desperately need that baptism of fire to fall on us today. Ask God for that baptism of Spirit and fire, and He will give it.

Extra:
Philemon 1:5-7

"Hearing of thy love and faith, which thou hast toward the Lord Jesus, and toward all saints; ⁶That the communication of thy faith may become effectual by the acknowledging of every good thing which is in you in Christ Jesus. ⁷For we have great joy and consolation in thy love, because the bowels of the saints are refreshed by thee, brother."

Paul commends Philemon for the love that he shows toward the saints. Philemon's love is evident because it has an effect of refreshing the saints. As a pastor, permit me to tell you something I know by experience. The easiest people to pastor are those who do have a strong love for God and the saints. The reason is because they all refresh one another.

June 3
Read: I Kings 20; Hebrews 2-4

Hebrews 4:12
"For the word of God is quick, and powerful, and sharper than any twoedged sword, piercing even to the dividing asunder of soul and spirit, and of the joints and marrow, and is a discerner of the thoughts and intents of the heart."

There is nothing in this world that has such an effect on men as the preaching of the gospel of Christ, but we must keep it sharp. In my high school wood shop class, I was taught that we are to always keep our tools sharp. The duller a tool is, the more effort you have to put forth. The sharper the tool, the less effort it takes to accomplish your task. The sharper the ax, the less swings you have to take. So too, if we keep the word of God sharp it will take less effort to produce life. The sharp edge is taken off the word of God by downplaying truth and depending on the intellect. Thus, the more effort man will have to put forth to make disciples of all nations. No wonder there is so much burn out in the ministry today. Saints, keep your Bible sharp.

June 4
Read: I Kings 21; Hebrews 5-6

I Kings 21:20
"And Ahab said to Elijah, Hast thou found me, O mine enemy? And he answered, I have found thee: because thou hast sold thyself to work evil in the sight of the LORD."

It is usually those who aren't living for the Lord like they should be that are the ones who can't get along with anyone in the church. They see everyone as their enemy. No peace with God, no peace with man.

June 5
Read: I Kings 22; Hebrews 7-8

I Kings 22:15-16
"So he came to the king. And the king said unto him, Micaiah, shall we go against Ramothgilead to battle, or shall we forbear? And he answered him, Go, and prosper: for the LORD shall deliver it into the hand of the king. ¹⁶And the king said unto him, **How many times shall I adjure thee that thou tell me nothing but that which is true in the name of the LORD?**"

Even a man or woman of God, at times, can speak according to his own mind. Don't be fooled, even people who don't live right or serve God somehow know when someone is speaking for God or not.

June 6
Read: II Kings 1-2; Hebrews 9-10

Hebrews 10:25
"Not forsaking the assembling of ourselves together, as the manner of some is; but exhorting one another: and so much the more, as ye see the day approaching."

One of the reasons some Christians don't appreciate assembling together with the saints is because they haven't been beaten up by this world yet. Friendship with the world makes one comfortable in the world. But the more you love Christ, the more this world will despise you and persecute you. Then the assembling with the saints becomes a refuge from the world and a wonderful place to be.

June 7
Read: II Kings 3-4; Hebrews 11

Hebrews 11:29
*"By faith they passed through the Red Sea as by dry land: which the **Egyptians assaying to do were drowned**."*

Faith is more than just believing God to do a miracle; faith is also walking in and through that miracle. When Egypt tried to walk through it they drowned. The world cannot walk where faithful believers walk.

June 8
Read: II Kings 5-6; Hebrews 12

Hebrews 12:14
"Follow peace with all men, and holiness, without which no man shall see the Lord."

The Bible teaches us to put on the new man, put on Christ and put on the whole armor. The Bible does not tell us to put on holiness. We are to follow after and live a holy life. Though you can dress in an unholy way, you cannot dress to make yourself holy. To try to do that is actually an insult against God. It degrades and takes from the severity of His holiness to think man can just throw on an outfit and that it now puts him on par with God's holiness.

June 9
Read: II Kings 7-8; Hebrews 13

Hebrews 13:12
"Wherefore Jesus also, that he might sanctify the people with his own blood, suffered without the gate."

The instant you were born again, you changed from a vile, rebellious, sin-laden person into a holy saint of God. I know you didn't even get a chance to act holy those few moments after your conversion, but nonetheless the blood of Christ made you holy. This is called positional holiness. After that initial conversion, the blood continues to work in your life to cause you to walk a holy life. This is called progressive holiness. Praise God, the blood sanctifies you and helps you to walk a sanctified life.

June 10
Read: II Kings 9-10; James 1-2

James 1:2-4
"My brethren, count it all joy when ye fall into divers temptations; ³Knowing this, that the trying of your faith worketh patience. ⁴But let patience have her perfect work, **that ye may be perfect** *and entire, wanting nothing."*

When Christians face trials there will be other Christians who will say things to them like; "You are facing that trial because something is wrong in your life," or, "Brother, you have sin in your life." They say it with an attitude like "that's what you get." When it really comes down to it, we do face trials because there is something wrong in our life. It is often not because we are living in sin or rebellion, it is just God removing our imperfections. None of us need to be offended by what I am saying, for this is what the scriptures teach; *"… that ye may be perfect…"* TRIALS PURGE US TO PERFECTION. HALLELUJAH!

June 11
Read: II Kings 11-12; James 3-4

James 4:8
"Draw nigh to God, and he will draw nigh to you. Cleanse your hands, ye sinners; and purify your hearts, ye double minded."

There is a message that has made its way into many churches today that promotes spiritual laziness and discourages an active vibrant pursuit of God. This false message teaches that our Christianity is based on a reaction to what God does in our life. It teaches that any attempt to surrender to the Lordship of Jesus Christ and endeavor to live a life that pleases God is legalism. But notice the order that James lays out. He does not say, if God draws nigh to us, we will draw nigh to Him; he says, if we draw nigh to God, then He will draw nigh to us. Yes saints, pursue Him with all your might. That's not legalism, in fact, there are no rules at all that forbid you to pursue Him with all your might.

June 12
Read: II Kings 13-14; James 5 - I Peter 1

II Kings 13:20-21
"Then Elisha died, and they buried him. And the raiding bands from Moab invaded the land in the spring of the year. ²¹So it was, as they were burying a man, that suddenly they spied a band of raiders; and they put the man in the tomb of Elisha; and when the man was let down and touched the bones of Elisha, he revived and stood on his feet."

A true man or woman of God has an effect on people, not just while they are living but even after they die. In fact, all the writers of our Bible have had a bigger effect in this world after they were dead then while they were living. Billions of people for thousands of years have read what these men have done and what they have written down. The effect that they made brings forth life. When that dead man's body touched the bones of Elisha, who was dead as well, the man came to life. You cannot hold life down. When it looks as if it is all over with, when death seems to be all around, do not be discouraged, for the life of Christ can and will rise up and touch the desperate soul. Life will spring forth.

June 13
Read: II Kings 15-16; I Peter 2-3

I Peter 2:17
"Honour all men. Love the brotherhood. Fear God. Honour the king."

Some say, I don't have to go to church to be a Christian, so why should I go? So you can *"love the brotherhood,"* that's one good reason why.

June 14
Read: II Kings 17; I Peter 3-4

I Peter 4:17
*"For the time is come that judgment must begin at the house of God: and if it first **begin at us**, what shall the end be of them that obey not the gospel of God?"*

If judgment begins with us, then I must realize that for me personally, it starts with me. This is the one time, before God, that I can and must put myself first. If I let the Holy Spirit continually judge my life, I will not be so eager to judge anyone else's life; but when I do, it will be a righteous judgment meant for their spiritual well-being.

June 15
Read: II Kings 18-19; I Peter 5 – II Peter 1

II Kings 19:6
*"And Isaiah said unto them, Thus shall ye say to your master, Thus saith the LORD, **Be not afraid of the words** which thou hast heard, with which the servants of the king of Assyria have blasphemed me."*

We sure hear a lot of bad news today. We are bombarded with lies from people and the devil. We hear all kinds of gossip and rumors. Words, words, words, all around us. Do you fear those words? Do you fear all the bad news you hear? *"Thus saith the LORD, Be not afraid of the words..."* God has revealed His love and care for us, yet we so easily get discouraged by words. Talk is cheap; God's love for us is real and He watches over us. If per chance, you want to continue to fear words, how about fearing the WORD of the LORD.

June 16
Read: II Kings 20-21; II Peter 2-3

II Peter 2:19
"While they promise them liberty, they themselves are the servants of corruption: **for of whom a man is overcome, of the same is he brought in bondage.**"

If we subject ourselves to this world, we will be overcome by it; but if we subject ourselves to the Spirit, we will be overcome by Him. The world brings bondage, the Spirit brings liberty. So the secret to being an overcomer is being overcome by the Spirit, *"… be filled with the Spirit"* (Ephesians 5:18).

June 17
Read: II Kings 22-23; I John 1-2

II Kings 22:10-11
"And Shaphan the scribe shewed the king, saying, Hilkiah the priest hath delivered me a book. And Shaphan read it before the king. ¹¹And it came to pass, when the king had heard the words of the book of the law, that he rent his clothes."

The king who is being referred to was King Josiah. The only example that was available for the young King Josiah was to walk the way his great, great, great … grandfather David did. You don't know it until you read, that the book of the law was not available to him at first. It found a place on a shelf in the house of God just collecting dust, (sound familiar?). Anyway, from the start, Josiah had a heart for the Lord. He wanted to obey Him. Josiah sent some men to oversee repairs on the house of the Lord. While working on the house, the book of the law was discovered. It was read to King Josiah and it gripped his soul. How I long to see the word of God affect Christians again the way it did Josiah. If Christians will once again be willing to be governed by that book, if they will once again desire the paths of God like Josiah did, then the reading of the word of God will burst their soul wide open again. Hallelujah!

June 18
Read: II Kings 24-25; I John 3-4

I John 3:7
"Little children, let no man deceive you: he that doeth righteousness is righteous, even as he is righteous."

Attempting to live in righteousness does not make a person righteous. Righteousness is the life people who are made righteous live.

June 19
Read: I Chronicles 1-2; I John 5 - II John

I Chronicles 1:25
"Eber, Peleg, Reu."

This list of three names is the shortest verse in the Old Testament. These names got recorded in God's word just because they were part of a family genealogy. There is another book in heaven that will have names recorded in it. You can't get your name in it because of family roots; you can't even get your name in it if you are a big shot. It is a book called the "book of life" and only one family gets their name recorded in it, the family of God, those who are sons of God. That includes daughters too.

June 20
Read: I Chronicles 3-4; III John – Jude

Jude 1:4
*"For there are certain men crept in unawares, who were before of old ordained to this condemnation, ungodly men, turning the grace of our God into lasciviousness, and **denying the only Lord** God, and our **Lord** Jesus Christ."*

It appears some Christians teach or are taught that Christians can willfully live in sin and that Jesus does not have to be your Lord, but you still will go to heaven. They believe none of that matters just as long as you accept the grace of God. However, grace isn't about God accepting us in our sin, grace is God delivering us from our sin. Grace isn't about God accepting you for who you are, God's grace delivers you from who you are.

June 21
Read: I Chronicles 5-6; Revelation 1-2

Revelation 1:9
"I John, who also am your brother, and companion in tribulation, and in the kingdom and patience of Jesus Christ, was in the isle that is called Patmos, for the word of God, and for the testimony of Jesus Christ."

If you declare the word of God as the absolute truth and if you have a strong testimony of Jesus Christ, then at times you will feel like you are on an island. It will be and has always been, that the more you pursue Christ, the less people there are who will join you.

June 22
Read: I Chronicles 7-8; Revelation 3-4

Revelation 3:15-19
"I know thy works, that thou art neither cold nor hot: I would thou wert cold or hot. ^{16}So then because thou art lukewarm, and neither cold nor hot, I will spue thee out of my mouth. ^{17}Because thou sayest, I am rich, and increased with goods, and have need of nothing; and

knowest not** that thou art wretched, and miserable, and poor, and blind, and naked:* ¹⁸*I counsel thee to buy of me gold tried in the fire, that thou mayest be rich; and white raiment, that thou mayest be clothed, and that the shame of thy nakedness do not appear;* ***and anoint thine eyes with eyesalve, that thou mayest see."

The reason the Laodicean church was lukewarm is because they had an inability to discern their spiritual condition. They thought everything was fine. They thought they had an outstanding reputation as Christians, yet Jesus is warning them to repent because they did not see their real spiritual state. God would never rebuke a man for being physically blind, but He does hold every Christian responsible for their spiritual eyesight. No one will ever be able to stand before God and say, "Sorry Lord, I just didn't see that. Lord, I didn't know that I was spiritually naked before you." There is an epidemic in the church in America, it is a refusal to want to have spiritual eyesight. Christians want to be left alone with the level of Christianity that they live at. They know in their heart that they are responsible to live in the light that is revealed to them, so they would just as soon stay in darkness. But God calls this "lukewarm," and the future for these people, unless they repent, is to be vomited out of God's mouth. It is not too late to call on God to open your eyes. Ask Him for an ever increasing revelation of Christ. He will give you eyesalve, but you must anoint your eyes with it. You must want to see.

June 23
Read: I Chronicles 9-10; Revelation 5-6

I Chronicles 10:4
*"Then said Saul to his armourbearer, Draw thy sword, and thrust me through therewith; lest **these uncircumcised** come and abuse me. But his armourbearer would not; for he was sore afraid. So Saul took a sword, and fell upon it."*

The worst tragedy of Saul's life is that he was alive long enough to make amends with the Lord, but instead he only saw the uncircumcised Philistines instead of the merciful loving Lord. If your heart is uncircumcised, you will only see the uncircumcised.

June 24
Read: I Chronicles 11-12; Revelation 7-8

I Chronicles 12:21-22
"And they helped David against the band of the rovers: for they were all mighty men of valour, and were captains in the host. ²²For at that time day by day there came to David to help him, until it was a great host, like the host of God."

David was one of the greatest leaders and kings in all of history. Great leaders attract great followers. There is no one, at least recorded in the Bible, who had the mighty men of valor helping like David did. Great leaders are made great by faithful followers. Faithful followers start by following after God. If a pastor wants God's sheep to be easy to lead, then he must show them how to follow after God.

June 25
Read: I Chronicles 13-15; Revelation 9-10

Revelation 10:6
*"And sware by him that liveth for ever and ever, who created heaven, and the things that therein are, and the earth, and the things that therein are, and the sea, and the things which are therein, that there **should be time no longer**."*

Other versions of this verse say that there should no more be a delay. As for now, the Lord is delaying His coming. Do not get so caught up in this world that you live like the Lord is always going to delay His return. One day the trump will sound and there will no more be a delay.

June 26
Read: I Chronicles 16-17; Revelation 11-12

Revelation 12:9
"And the great dragon was cast out, that old serpent, called the Devil, and Satan, which deceiveth the whole world: he was cast out into the earth, and his angels were cast out with him."

Satan was overcome in heaven and he can be overcome on earth. Not by all, but by those who have the kingdom of heaven in their heart. Satan cannot overcome where God's kingdom is.

June 27
Read: I Chronicles 18-20; Revelation 13-14

I Chronicles 20:8
"These were born unto the giant in Gath; and they fell by the hand of David, and by the hand of his servants."

Just because you conquered one giant, doesn't mean there won't be more you will have to face. Once you conquer one through the power of the Spirit, it may not mean the next giant will go down easier, but at least it should boost your faith to know the next one will fall too.

June 28
Read: I Chronicles 21-22; Revelation 15-16

I Chronicles 22:5
"And David said, Solomon my son is young and tender, and the house that is to be builded for the LORD must be exceeding magnifical, of fame and of glory throughout all countries: I will therefore now make preparation for it. So David prepared abundantly before his death."

King David, before his death, ordered stone to be hewn and cedar to be gathered and nails to be made from iron, all for the construction of the temple. You could say he was concerned about how the next generation would build. So too, must the church and ministry today have the same concern for the next generation and prepare them to lead and minister to the church, the living breathing house of the Lord.

June 29
Read: I Chronicles 23-25; Revelation 17-18

Revelation 17:1-4
"And there came one of the seven angels which had the seven vials, and talked with me, saying unto me, Come hither; I will shew unto thee the judgment of the great whore that sitteth upon many waters: ²With whom the kings of the earth have committed fornication, and the inhabitants of the earth have been made drunk with the wine of her fornication. ³So he carried me away in the spirit into the wilderness: and I saw a woman sit upon a scarlet coloured beast, full of names of blasphemy, having seven heads and ten horns. ⁴And the woman was arrayed in purple and scarlet colour, and decked with gold and precious stones and pearls, having a golden cup in her hand full of abominations and filthiness of her fornication."

The harlot church of our day is growing. Her grand finale will be when she becomes the one world religion of the tribulation period. By then the whole world will be given over to her fornications. They will be impressed with her royal purple and scarlet colors, they will trust in her gold, precious stones and pearls. Yes she looks glamourous, but her path is the way to hell. If you remain with the present day harlot church system, you are setting yourself up for the most powerful of deceptions.

June 30
Read: I Chronicles 26-27; Revelation 19-20

Revelation 19:7
"Let us be glad and rejoice, and give honour to him: for the marriage of the Lamb is come, and his wife hath made herself ready."

Noah prepared an ark because he was expecting rain. Joseph stored grain because he was expecting a famine. Joshua and the army of Israel shouted because they expected the walls to fall down. David took five smooth stones because he was expecting to defeat a giant. Christians will make themselves ready, if they are expecting the Lord to return to take them to the marriage supper of the Lamb.

July

July 1
Read: I Chronicles 28-29; Revelation 21

I Chronicles 29:5
*"The gold for things of gold, and the silver for things of silver, and for **all manner of work** to be made by the hands of artificers. And who then is **willing to consecrate** his service this day unto the LORD?"*

The problem with too many Christians is that they think that since they are not called to be a minister in the church, they don't need to be consecrated.

Extra:
I Chronicles 29:17
*"I know also, my God, that thou **triest the heart, and hast pleasure in uprightness**. As for me, in the uprightness of mine heart I have willingly offered all these things: and now have I seen with joy thy people, which are present here, to offer willingly unto thee."*

We don't try God, He tries us. He doesn't try us to see if we will buckle under temptation and pressure, He tries us because it is His pleasure to find uprightness lodged in our heart.

July 2
Read: II Chronicles 1-3; Revelation 22

II Chronicles 2:8-9
"Send me also cedar trees, fir trees, and algum trees, out of Lebanon: for I know that thy servants can skill to cut timber in Lebanon; and, behold, my servants shall be with thy servants, ⁹Even to prepare me timber in abundance: for the house which I am about to build shall be wonderful great."

With great enthusiasm Solomon determined to build a temple unto God. It took thousands of men and a great amount of gold and other metals. Most, if not all of us, could not build such a temple because we have not the money nor the man power. However, there is not one of us that can't afford to provide a temple for the Holy Spirit. All He requires is you, whether rich or poor, healthy or sick, tall or short and male or female.

July 3
Read: II Chronicles 4-6; Matthew 1-2

II Chronicles 5:1
*"Thus all the work that Solomon made for the house of the LORD was finished: and **Solomon brought in all the things that David his father had dedicated**; and the silver, and the gold, and all the instruments, put he among the treasures of the house of God."*

Though it is of the utmost importance that each of us have our own testimony and relationship with the Lord, there is value in remembering what the dedicated ones who walked before us contributed to the body of Christ. When we remember what they gave us, it should encourage us to leave behind a dedicated life as well.

July 4
Read: II Chronicles 7-8; Matthew 3-4

Matthew 4:6-7, 10-11
"And saith unto him, If thou be the Son of God, cast thyself down: for it is written, He shall give his angels charge concerning thee: and in their hands they shall bear thee up, lest at any time thou dash thy foot against a stone. [7]Jesus said unto him, It is written again, Thou shalt not tempt the Lord thy God... [10]Then saith Jesus unto him, Get thee hence, Satan: for it is written, Thou shalt worship the Lord thy God, and him only shalt thou serve. [11]Then the devil leaveth him, and, behold, angels came and ministered unto him."

Those who believe the Bible will overcome them who just quote the Bible.

July 5
Read: II Chronicles 9-10; Matthew 5

II Chronicles 9:1
"And when the queen of Sheba heard of the fame of Solomon, she came to prove Solomon with hard questions at Jerusalem, with a very great company, and camels that bare spices, and gold in abundance, and precious stones: and when she was come to Solomon, she communed with him of all that was in her heart."

The queen came prepared to give in abundance, if the report she heard was true. The report was true and she gave it. She didn't visit Solomon to get more of the things of this world that she already had, she went to get what the world can't offer. This is why the church must stop offering worldly ministry to the lost. They don't need more of what they have, they need what they don't have, CHRIST.

July 6
Read: II Chronicles 11-13; Matthew 6

II Chronicles 12:6-7, 12
*"Whereupon the princes of Israel and **the king humbled themselves**; and they said, The LORD is righteous. ⁷And when the LORD saw that they humbled themselves, the word of the LORD came to Shemaiah, saying, They have humbled themselves; therefore I will not destroy them, but I will grant them some deliverance; and my wrath shall not be poured out upon Jerusalem by the hand of Shishak... ¹²And when **he humbled himself**, the wrath of the LORD turned from him, that he would not destroy him altogether: and also in Judah things went well."*

I am sure every sincere Christian wants to do great things for God. The king who is being referred to in this portion of scripture is King Rehoboam. He doesn't have a record of doing anything great, but he did protect Jerusalem from the enemy. He didn't do it by military strength. He didn't do it by signing peace treaties. He did it by humbling himself. It could be that one of the greatest things we will ever do for the kingdom of God is humble ourselves.

July 7
Read: II Chronicles 14-16; Matthew 7

Matthew 7:13-14
"Enter ye in at the strait gate: for wide is the gate, and broad is the way, that leadeth to destruction, and many there be which go in thereat: ¹⁴Because **strait is the gate***, and* **narrow is the way***, which leadeth unto life, and few there be that find it."*

Jesus the Savior is the straight gate; Jesus the Lord is the narrow way.

July 8
Read: II Chronicles 17-18; Matthew 8

II Chronicles 18:11-12
"And all the prophets prophesied so, saying, Go up to Ramothgilead, and prosper: for the LORD shall deliver it into the hand of the king. ¹²And the messenger that went to call Micaiah spake to him, saying, Behold, **the words of the prophets declare good** *to the king with one assent; let thy word therefore, I pray thee, be like one of theirs, and speak thou good."*

Preacher of truth, the odds are stacked against you. The pressure is on like never before to *"declare good"* to everyone like the false Prophets do and to let your words be like theirs. However, though the odds are against you, God is with you and for you, and when the smoke has cleared, the truth will still be standing. Saints, we are just about out of time. Let the truth be known like never before, and whosoever will receive the truth will stand with it and on it.

July 9
Read: II Chronicles 19-21; Matthew 9

II Chronicles 20:35-37
"And after this did Jehoshaphat king of Judah join himself with Ahaziah king of Israel, who did very wickedly: ³⁶And he joined himself with him to make ships to go to Tarshish: and they made the

ships in Eziongeber. ³⁷Then Eliezer the son of Dodavah of Mareshah prophesied against Jehoshaphat, saying, **Because thou hast joined thyself with Ahaziah, the LORD hath broken thy works.** *And the ships were broken, that they were not able to go to Tarshish."*

There is a call throughout America for the church to put aside her differences and join together as one. Paul commanded that there should be no division amongst us; yet, God sent a prophet to rebuke Jehoshaphat for joining himself with the king of Israel, even though they both had Jewish blood. Saints, same with us, we don't join together with just anyone who calls themselves a Christian; we join ourselves to Christ. All those who are truly in Christ will join together. By the way, those that are in Christ will have fellowship; those who are not in Christ will have broken-ship.

July 10
Read: II Chronicles 22-23; Matthew 10

Matthew 10:34
"Think not that I am come to send peace on earth: I came not to send peace, but a sword."

Jesus came to bring a sword instead of peace. What kind of Prince of Peace is He? Now that the question was asked, I will answer it. After closer reading, you will see that He is talking about peace on earth. The peace He brings is peace to the inner man. It is this kind of peace that calms you while this world spins out of control. Church, most of us know the Savior side of Jesus, many know the Lord side of Jesus, but the day is right around the corner that we will see the Prince of Peace side of Jesus like never before. When judgment and destruction come, you will know and learn His peace and you will give glory to the PRINCE OF PEACE.

July 11
Read: II Chronicles 24-25; Matthew 11

II Chronicles 25:10
"Then Amaziah separated them, to wit, the army that was come to him out of Ephraim, to go home again: wherefore their anger was greatly kindled against Judah, and they returned home in great anger."

There will be a time when the church will be engaged in a great work for the kingdom of God. That work will be hindered by believers who have not been serious with God, but all of a sudden want to participate. They must be kept from participating, at least until they are in the right spirit, for our work is a spiritual work.

July 12
Read: II Chronicles 26-28; Matthew 12

II Chronicles 28:6
"For Pekah the son of Remaliah slew in Judah an hundred and twenty thousand in one day, **which were all valiant men**; *because they had forsaken the LORD God of their fathers."*

These were valiant men of Judah who were slain, which teaches us that being valiant, talented, clever, wise, strong or noble does you no good if you have forsaken the Lord.

July 13
Read: II Chronicles 29-30; Matthew 13

Matthew 13:15
"For the hearts of this people have grown dull. Their ears are hard of hearing, and their eyes they have closed, lest they should see with their eyes and hear with their ears, lest they should understand with their hearts and turn, so that I should heal them" (NKJV).

A dull heart stops up ears and closes eyes.

July 14
Read: II Chronicles 31-32; Matthew 14

II Chronicles 32:13-14
"Know ye not what I and my fathers have done unto all the people of other lands? were the gods of the nations of those lands any ways able to deliver their lands out of mine hand? Who was there among all the gods of those nations that my fathers utterly destroyed, that could deliver his people out of mine hand, **that your God should be able to deliver you out of mine hand***?"*

This is what the servant of the King of Syria shouted out to Hezekiah and Judah as they prepared for war. Syria saw every nation's god the same, weak and inferior. Church, does the world see our God as just another god of a religion? Do they see our God no different than other gods? If the heavens declare the glory of God, I think it is about time we, the church, start to declare and demonstrate the glory of God.

July 15
Read: II Chronicles 33-34; Matthew 15

Matthew 15:26-27
"But he answered and said, It is not meet to take the children's bread, and to cast it to dogs. ^{27}And she said, Truth, Lord: **yet the dogs eat of the crumbs** *which fall from their masters' table."*

This foreign, Syrophenician woman believed there was more power in Jesus' leftovers than much of the church believes for the power in the gourmet.

July 16
Read: II Chronicles 35-36; Matthew 16-17

Matthew 16:9-11
"Do ye not yet **understand***, neither remember the five loaves of the five thousand, and how many baskets ye took up? ^{10}Neither the seven*

*loaves of the four thousand, and how many baskets ye took up? ¹¹How is it that ye do not **understand** that I spake it not to you concerning bread, that ye should beware of the leaven of the Pharisees and of the Sadducees?"*

I am sure all of us have those moments of frustration when we have a hard time understanding portions of scriptures. Just imagine if you could personally sit down with Jesus and ask Him your questions, you would think that He would explain everything so simple. Well, His disciples often sat down with Him and asked Him questions, but they too were left without understanding. Don't be frustrated, be content with what you already know and walk in that. You will get more understanding as you are faithful to walk in the light you already received. Don't grasp for what you don't have, live in what you do. After all, if you could figure out everything about God, He wouldn't be very big.

July 17
Read: Ezra 1-2; Matthew 18

Matthew 18:3-4
*"And said, Verily I say unto you, Except ye be converted, and become **as little children**, ye shall not enter into the kingdom of heaven. ⁴Whosoever therefore shall humble himself as this little child, the same is greatest in the kingdom of heaven."*

Perpetual childhood is the path to greatness in heaven. It doesn't say "as little babies," but "*as little children.*" Some Christians need to grow up and quit being babies, but not grow out of being as little children in their faith.

July 18
Read: Ezra 3-4; Matthew 19-20

Ezra 3:1
"And when the seventh month was come, and the children of Israel were in the cities, the people gathered themselves together as one man to Jerusalem."

Our generation will begin to understand what the church really is when the believers gather themselves together as one man. That one man must be Christ.

July 19
Read: Ezra 5-6; Matthew 21

Ezra 5:1-2
"Then the prophets, Haggai the prophet, and Zechariah the son of Iddo, prophesied unto the Jews that were in Judah and Jerusalem in the name of the God of Israel, even unto them.² Then rose up Zerubbabel the son of Shealtiel, and Jeshua the son of Jozadak, and began to build the house of God which is at Jerusalem: **and with them were the prophets of God helping them**.*"*

The Lord spoke to the Jews through the prophet Haggai; *"Go up to the mountain, and bring wood, and build the house; and I will take pleasure in it, and I will be glorified, saith the LORD"* (Haggai 1:8). Haggai didn't just tell them what God said, but he went with them. A true man of God would never preach, teach or give orders to do something unless he was living it himself and it was in his heart to do.

July 20
Read: Ezra 7-8; Matthew 22

Ezra 7:10
"For Ezra had prepared his heart to seek the law of the LORD, and ***to do it, and to teach*** *in Israel statutes and judgments."*

Notice the order of Ezra's heart? Seek, do and teach. If you teach before you do, you're a hypocrite; if you do before you seek, you're religious. It is in seeking the Lord that the will of the Lord is known. Then the doing can happen, then follows the teaching. Jesus followed this same pattern. *"The former treatise have I made, O Theophilus, of all that Jesus began both to* ***do and teach***,*"* (Acts 1:1).

July 21
Read: Ezra 9-10; Matthew 23-24

Matthew 24:37-39
"But as the days of Noe were, so shall also the coming of the Son of man be. ^{38}For as in the days that were before the flood they were eating and drinking, marrying and giving in marriage, until the day that Noe entered into the ark, ^{39}And knew not until the flood came, and took them all away; so shall also the coming of the Son of man be."

Jesus gave us huge glimpse of what the last of the last days would be like by telling us they will be like the days of Noah. All we need to do is go back to the book of Genesis and read about it for ourselves. Here are some of the similarities that can be found between Noah's generation and ours.
- *"But Noah found grace in the eyes of the LORD"* (Genesis 6:8). We found it too in this age of grace.
- Life will go on as usual.
- Noah knew the flood was coming but the wicked did not. *"But ye brethren are not in darkness, that the day should overtake you as a thief"* (I Thessalonians 5:5).
- Noah had a call. We have men who are called today.
- Noah was part of a great minority. The way is still narrow that leads to life and few find it.
- Building the ark was an act of faith. We are saved by grace through faith.
- Noah built the ark in the presence of a sin gripped world. In the last days iniquity shall abound. Noah built the ark in a time when *"the wickedness of man was great in the earth, and that every imagination of the thoughts of his heart was only evil continually"* (Genesis 6:5).
- Noah was a preacher of righteousness. Are you?

July 22
Read: Nehemiah 1-2; Matthew 25

Nehemiah 1:1-4
*"The words of Nehemiah the son of Hachaliah. And it came to pass in the month Chisleu, in the twentieth year, as I was in Shushan the palace, ²That Hanani, one of my brethren, came, he and certain men of Judah; and **I asked them concerning the Jews that had escaped**, which were left of the captivity, and concerning Jerusalem. ³And they said unto me, **The remnant that are left of the captivity there in the province are in great affliction and reproach**: the wall of Jerusalem also is broken down, and the gates thereof are burned with fire. ⁴And it came to pass, when I heard these words, that **I sat down and wept, and mourned certain days, and fasted, and prayed before the God of heaven.**"*

Has anyone recognized the state of the church here in America? She thinks she has *"need of nothing."* It seems few recognize the great affliction she is in; affliction not from persecution but from comfort and prosperity. Much of the church is in survival mode. Does anyone have a burden for Christ's church like Nehemiah had for the Jews? Are any of you saints willing to fast and pray and step out to lead your brethren to the high call of the Lord Jesus Christ? Or are you just surviving as well?

July 23
Read: Nehemiah 3-4; Matthew 26

Matthew 26:28
"For this is my blood of the <u>new testament</u>, which is shed for many for the remission of sins."

The blood of Christ transitioned us from the old covenant to the new, from the Old Testament to the New. After Jesus spilt His blood and rose from the dead, there was no longer any need for the Old Testament ministry of the high priest sprinkling the blood of a slain lamb on behalf of men's sin. At best, the blood of bulls and goats was a temporary covering for sin. The ministry of the high priest was a constant reminder to fallen man of his bondage to sin. However,

Jesus changed all that with His blood. That one time sacrifice of the blood from the final High Priest, Jesus Christ, is more than a temporary covering. It is the antidote for full forgiveness of sin, and even more, it is power over sin. The blood forgives us, the blood empowers us to no longer have to be in bondage to sin. Thank you God, for offering up Your Lamb of God.

July 24
Read: Nehemiah 5-6; Matthew 27:1-44

Matthew 27:29-31
"And when they had platted a crown of thorns, they put it upon his head, and a reed in his right hand: and they bowed the knee before him, and **mocked him***, saying, Hail, King of the Jews! ³⁰And they spit upon him, and took the reed, and smote him on the head. ³¹And after that they had* **mocked him***, they took the robe off from him, and put his own raiment on him, and led him away to crucify him."*

Jesus was mocked because He was hated by this world. His presence brought strong conviction and therefore this world could not handle Him. Today much of the church is mocked, but I fear it is not because of the righteous standard she brings, but because of her failing to be the representation of Christ. We constantly hear of ministers falling into sexual sin and financial misdealing and our society can't help but mock the church for her failure to uphold her integrity. Church, there is no way out of it, you are going to be mocked; you must decide if it is because of the absence of Christ in you and the hypocrisy on display or the evidence of Christ in you and the righteousness that flows from your life.

July 25
Read: Nehemiah 7-8; Matthew 27:45 – 28

Nehemiah 8:10
"Then he said unto them, Go your way, eat the fat, and drink the sweet, and send portions unto them for whom nothing is prepared: for this day is holy unto our Lord: neither be ye sorry; for **the joy of the LORD is your strength***."*

Some Christians lack strength because they lack joy. They must remember that the kingdom of God is *"righteousness, peace and joy in the Holy Ghost."*

July 26
Read: Nehemiah 9; Mark 1

Mark 1:22
"And they were astonished at his doctrine: for he taught them as one that had authority, and not as the scribes."

Give a man a teaching outline and he can teach doctrine. Get a man filled with the Holy Ghost and he can astonish you with doctrine.

July 27
Read: Nehemiah 10-11; Mark 2

Mark 2:17
"When Jesus heard it, he saith unto them, They that are whole have no need of the physician, but they that are sick: I came not to call the righteous, but sinners to repentance."

I am sure that almost 100% of those who are dying of cancer would be delighted to hear that a doctor was coming to see them at no charge, and that he was going to minister a drug that was positively going to cure them and leave them very healthy. Yet mankind is chronically sick with sin, and hell's mouth is open wide to swallow them up with eternal destruction, yet few seem to rejoice over the good news that Jesus will deliver them and heal them of their chronic sin problem. Maybe the church has failed to accurately diagnose those who come to visit and tell them the truth about their condition. Maybe Christians have done a disservice by trying to comfort and soothe the sinner which leaves him unaware of just how sick and full of sin disease he is. Unless man knows how lost and desperate he is, he will never be looking for a Savior. Please, do not fear those who will accuse you of being judgmental, because you want to help the sinner see his spiritual condition so he can call on the name of the Lord Jesus Christ and be saved. Help the sinner know the bad news, so that he can love the good news.

July 28
Read: Nehemiah 12-13; Mark 3

Mark 3:13-15
*"And he goeth up into a mountain, and calleth unto him whom he would: and they came unto him. ¹⁴And he ordained twelve, that **they should be with him**, and that he might send them forth to preach, ¹⁵And to have power to heal sicknesses, and to cast out devils."*

In verse 14, Jesus taught a very simple, most often neglected principle. He ordained twelve men that they first *"should be with Him,"* then follows the sending out and the power to accompany their work. Being with and knowing Him must precede preaching Him.

July 29
Read: Esther 1-2; Mark 4

Mark 4:26-29
"And he said, So is the kingdom of God, as if a man should cast seed into the ground; ²⁷And should sleep, and rise night and day, and the seed should spring and grow up, he knoweth not how. ²⁸For the earth bringeth forth fruit of herself; first the blade, then the ear, after that the full corn in the ear. ²⁹But when the fruit is brought forth, immediately he putteth in the sickle, because the harvest is come."

If you planted seed in a garden that had plenty of good moist soil, you would expect that which you planted to grow. It is only natural that the plants should grow and bring forth its flower or fruit. You would be more surprised if the plants didn't grow, then if they did. So too with the Christian, God has everything set in order that is needed for the Christian to grow. It should be just as alarming when a Christian doesn't grow as it is if a plant doesn't grow. If a Christian does not grow it is because something was disturbed. It means the Christian is working against the principles of growth. It actually takes more effort for a Christian to not grow because he would have to fight against that which happens naturally. There is a lot more turmoil in the Christian's life that resists God, then the Christian that resists sin and the devil. If you want to grow you must stay firmly planted and grounded in Christ and it will be impossible not to grow.

July 30
Read: Esther 3-5; Mark 5

Esther 4:1-2
"When Mordecai perceived all that was done, **Mordecai rent his clothes, and put on sackcloth with ashes,** *and went out into the midst of the city, and cried with a loud and a bitter cry;* ^{2}*And came even before the king's gate:* **for none might enter into the king's gate clothed with sackcloth.**"

See the difference between earthly kings and our heavenly King of kings? Mordecai was not permitted to enter King Ahasuerus's gate in that humble broken position. On the other hand, it is only in a humble position and attitude that we can enter the gate of the King of kings.

July 31
Read: Esther 6-8; Mark 6

Esther 7:1,10, 8:1
"So the king and Haman came to banquet with Esther the queen.... ^{10}So they hanged Haman on the gallows that he had prepared for Mordecai. Then was the king's wrath pacified....^{1}On that day did the king Ahasuerus give the house of Haman the Jews' enemy unto Esther the queen..."

The final showdown is soon to take place. The king (Jesus), Haman (Satan) and Esther the queen (the bride of Christ), are all in one room. There, Esther pleads for the life of her people. Haman, a man who hated the Jews was a man who was promoted over all the officials, just as Satan who hates God's people was given this world to rule. There is coming a day when it will all come to a head. God will cast Satan into an eternal hell, and Christ the king will give His bride authority to rule and reign with Him. Be encouraged today oh saints of God.

August

August 1
Read: Esther 9-10; Mark 7

Mark 7:1-2
"Then came together unto him the Pharisees, and certain of the scribes, which came from Jerusalem. ²And when they saw some of his disciples eat bread with defiled, that is to say, with unwashen, hands, they found fault."

Christians are quite confused about the whole idea of judging the church. Paul, in I Corinthians 5:12-13, tells us we are to judge the church. Yet many Christians hate the whole principle of being judged. One reason being judged is so distasteful to some is because they may too often have been judged by someone with Pharisaical attitude. The Pharisees didn't judge Jesus' disciples by the scriptures, they judged them by their letter of the law and standards. Demanding Christians to line up with your rules and regulations, often just gives them a bad taste for any kind of judgment. However, Christians who live by the word of God will not get all bent out of shape when they are judged by the word and by God-fearing saints who minister the word.

August 2
Read: Job 1-4; Mark 8

Job 2:9
"Then said his wife unto him, Dost thou still retain thine integrity? curse God, and die."

In the midst of all Job's suffering, his wife noticed he retained his integrity. It is way more important what people see in you then what they say to you.

August 3
Read: Job 5-8; Mark 9

Mark 9:5-6
"*And Peter answered and said to Jesus, Master, it is good for us to be here:* **and let us make three tabernacles;** *one for thee, and one for Moses, and one for Elias. ⁶For he wist not what to say; for* **they were sore afraid**."

Peter was so afraid that he couldn't help but respond with something that he thought sounded spiritual. However, the fear of God, without broken humility and repentance, often is the catalyst for the establishment of religious tabernacles and rituals.

August 4
Read: Job 9-12; Mark 10

Mark 10:17-22
"*¹⁷And when he was gone forth into the way,* **there came one running, and kneeled to him**, *and asked him, Good Master, what shall I do that I may inherit eternal life? ¹⁸And Jesus said unto him, Why callest thou me good? there is none good but one, that is, God. ¹⁹Thou knowest the commandments, Do not commit adultery, Do not kill, Do not steal, Do not bear false witness, Defraud not, Honour thy father and mother. ²⁰And he answered and said unto him, Master, all these have I observed from my youth. ²¹Then* **Jesus beholding him loved him**, *and said unto him, One thing thou lackest: go thy way, sell whatsoever thou hast, and give to the poor, and thou shalt have treasure in heaven: and come, take up the cross, and follow me. ²²***And he was sad at that saying, and went away grieved***: for he had great possessions.*"

The rich young man in this story is like many in the church today. They come running and kneeling before Jesus with all kinds of enthusiasm. They can even feel the love Jesus has for them. But of course, Jesus never avoids dealing with the heart. Once Jesus spoke to the heart of this rich young man, the enthusiasm he had that caused him to run and kneel before Jesus, turned to sadness as he now left the presence of Jesus. He walked away with his head down because he wanted both his riches and Jesus, but it cannot be. We can never serve Jesus on our terms. He must have our whole heart, soul and mind.

August 5
Read: Job 13-16; Mark 11

Job 16:12
"I was at ease, but he hath broken me asunder: he hath also taken me by my neck, and shaken me to pieces, and set me up for his mark."

I don't know if there was ever a more broken man than Job. He also said, "My skin is broken, and become loathsome," and again, "My days are past, my purposes are broken off," You are in good company if you have a broken spirit. Abraham was broken when he agreed to slay his son. Jacob was broken at the River Jabbok. Joseph was broken in a pit and a prison. Moses was broken in the backside of the wilderness. Joshua was broken when he gave a good report to a fearful doubting people. David lived a broken life. Nehemiah was broken with news that the Jews were in distress and the walls of Jerusalem were broken down. Isaiah was broken when he saw God high and lifted up. Jeremiah was so broken, he is called the weeping prophet. Jonah was broken in the belly of a whale. Peter was broken at the crowing of a rooster. Paul was broken on the road to Damascus. Don't resist a broken life.

August 6
Read: Job 17-20; Mark 12

Mark 12:9
"What shall therefore the lord of the vineyard do? he will come and destroy the husbandmen, and will give the vineyard unto others."

Just think, when Jesus said that others would be given the vineyard, He was talking about you. God is trusting you, let Him receive the fruit from it.

August 7
Read: Job 21-24; Mark 13

Mark 13:31
"Heaven and earth shall pass away: but my words shall not pass away."

The effort by man to somehow make the word of God more relevant is just a symptom that somewhere in the heart of man he has considered the word of God to be a bit outdated. No one comes right out and says that, and often they don't even realize it, but it becomes very apparent that there is a loss of confidence that the word (without man adding his hundreds of ideas and inventions to it) isn't good enough anymore. But let me remind you that the word of God will still be standing strong on its own, long after man's ideas and inventions have passed away.

August 8
Read: Job 25-29; Mark 14

Mark 14:30
*"And Jesus saith unto him, Verily I say unto thee, That this day, even in this night, before the **cock crow twice**, thou shalt deny me thrice."*

Peter denied Jesus the first time and the cock crowed. Peter then denied Jesus a second and third time, and the cock crowed again. O Lord, make us so sensitive to the conviction of the Spirit that if we sin, we repent on the first crowing.

Extra
Job 29:22
"After my words they spake not again; and my speech dropped upon them."

It is only when a person speaks under the anointing of the Holy Spirit that words will fall heavy upon people.

August 9
Read: Job 30-32; Mark 15

Mark 15:31
"Likewise also the chief priests mocking said among themselves with the scribes, He saved others; himself he cannot save."

The chief priests and the scribes did recognize one thing about Jesus, they said it openly right there in front of Him. They said it in agreement amongst themselves that this Jesus *"saved others."* However, the same ones that recognized that Jesus saves others never realized they needed to be saved. Self righteous people could never imagine that they would need to be saved. To them, Jesus is for others. Hallelujah, aren't you glad you are one of the others?

August 10
Read: Job 33-35; Mark 16

Mark 16:1
"And when the sabbath was past, Mary Magdalene, and Mary the mother of James, and Salome, had bought sweet spices, that they might come and anoint him."

The two Marys came to the tomb with sweet smelling spices because they believed Jesus was dead and that His body would stink. What kind of attitude do you come to church with? One of a dead Christ or a living one? Are you expecting church to be a tomb or a place of life?

August 11
Read: Job 36-38; Luke 1:1-40

Job 38:25
"Who hath divided a watercourse for the overflowing of waters, or a way for the lightning of thunder."

Though a bolt of lightning may not be exactly straight, God does direct its path so it will hit the exact mark He intended. So too, even if you go a little crooked at times, if you completely trust the Lord with your life you will hit the exact mark He expects you to. Of course, that mark is Christ.

August 12
Read: Job 39-42; Luke 1:41-80

Luke 1:41
*"And it came to pass, that, when Elisabeth heard the salutation of Mary, **the babe leaped in her womb**; and Elisabeth was filled with the Holy Ghost."*

God forbid that any Christian would ever fall for the lie that a fetus is nothing more than a blob of flesh until it is born. John the Baptist while in his mother's womb, reacted to Jesus who was in Mary's womb, when she entered the house. Parents, don't ever think your children are to young to respond to Jesus, and don't ever think they are to young to get filled with the Spirit. For the angel Gabriel told Zacharias, *"For he shall be great in the sight of the Lord, and shall drink neither wine nor strong drink; and he shall be filled with the Holy Ghost, even from his mother's womb"* (Luke 1:15).

August 13
Read: Psalms 1-7; Luke 2

Luke 2:40
"And the child grew, and waxed strong in spirit, filled with wisdom: and the grace of God was upon him."

Sometimes we can have a hard time connecting grace to anything but salvation, especially when there is so much of the hyper-grace gospel being preached around us. Jesus did not need to be saved, yet God put His grace upon Him. This should give us a better idea that grace isn't just for the lost, but even believers need the continued grace of God in their life.

August 14
Read: Psalms 8-15; Luke 3

Psalm 12:6
"The words of the LORD are pure words: as silver tried in a furnace of earth, purified seven times."

Lord, grant to us that we may speak such pure words.

August 15
Read: Psalms 16-19; Luke 4

Psalm 16:11
"Thou wilt shew me the path of life: in thy presence is fulness of joy; at thy right hand there are pleasures for evermore."

The greatest purpose of man is to give glory to God. The greatest pleasure of man is to be in the presence of God.

Extra
Luke 4:32
"And they were astonished at his doctrine: for his word was with power."

Before Jesus was baptized in the Holy Spirit (when He was the age of twelve) Luke wrote, *"And all that heard him were astonished at his understanding and answers"* (Luke 2:47). After Jesus was filled with the Spirit, the people were astonished with His power. Are you filled with the Spirit?

August 16
Read: Psalms 20-25; Luke 5

Psalm 23:1-2
*"The LORD is my shepherd; I shall not want. ²**He maketh me to lie down in green pastures**: he leadeth me beside the still waters."*

Most reliable versions of the Bible use the word *"maketh"* or *"make,"* before the words *"me to lie down…."* This means that the normal course of our relationship with the Lord is we will be at rest. He causes this rest, He makes it happen. Have you laid down yet? Have you rested? If not, you have been working very hard at resisting God's rest. That is why you are tired.

August 17
Read: Psalms 26-31; Luke 6

Luke 6:22
*"Blessed are ye, when men shall hate you, and when **they shall separate you from their company**, and shall reproach you, and cast out your name as evil, for the Son of man's sake."*

Strong faithful believers never have a difficult time staying separate from the world, for the world excludes them from joining them.

August 18
Read: Psalms 32-35; Luke 7

Psalm 32:1
*"**Blessed** is he whose transgression is forgiven, whose sin is covered."*

Saints, I guess that is you and me. That should pretty much take care of any complaining we think we have to right to do. Blessed people have nothing to complain about.

August 19
Read: Psalms 36-38; Luke 8

Luke 8:1-3
"And it came to pass afterward, that he went throughout every city and village, preaching and shewing the glad tidings of the kingdom of God: and the twelve were with him, ²And certain women, which had been healed of evil spirits and infirmities, Mary called

Magdalene, out of whom went seven devils, ³And Joanna the wife of Chuza Herod's steward, and Susanna, and many others, which ministered unto him of their substance."

Mary Magdalene, Joanna, Susanna and others followed Jesus not to get fed, or see the miracles, but to minister unto Him with that which they had. We are so conditioned today to bombard heaven with all our needs and wants. But these ladies who ministered unto the Lord teach us today that we can do more than just follow Him, we can minister unto the Lord. What a thought, the Almighty God, maker of heaven and earth, gives us mere man the privilege to minister unto Him. Saints, let's bless Him.

August 20
Read: Psalms 39-42; Luke 9

Luke 9:18-20
*"And it came to pass, as he was alone praying, his disciples were with him: and he asked them, saying, Whom say the **people** that I am? ¹⁹They answering said, John the Baptist; but some say, Elias; and others say, that one of the old prophets is risen again. ²⁰ He said unto them, But whom say ye that I am? Peter answering said, The Christ of God."*

In Greek, the word that *"people"* was translated from means crowds or throngs. So Jesus was asking, who do the crowds say I am? They answered John, or Elijah or a prophet of old. I just wanted to remind you, church, that the crowds always get it wrong.

August 21
Read: Psalms 43-48; Luke 10

Luke 10:21
*"In that hour Jesus rejoiced in spirit, and said, I thank thee, O Father, Lord of heaven and earth, that thou hast hid these things from the wise and prudent, and **hast revealed them unto babes**: even so, Father; for so it seemed good in thy sight."*

The longer I walk with the Lord the more I see that few Christians ever get a real revelation of Christ. I am not talking about those out there that claim they have new revelations of Christ. I stay far from that crowd. What is a most troubling thing in our generation is the amount of ministers of the gospel who lack revelation knowledge, who just don't get it. If they don't live in continual revelation knowledge of this great Christ, how will they be able to minister to those who are under their ministry? Now let me pry a little. If you, the reader, do not understand what I am talking about when it comes to revelation knowledge, then you are lacking this revelation as well. Do I say that to belittle you and condemn you? Absolutely not! I say it to declare to you, it is the most exciting thing to live a life that flows with revelation knowledge of the Lord. Without an ongoing revelation of Christ, your Christian life is at best mediocre. So how do you get to that place where God gives a greater revelation of Himself? Become a babe. If you are on a high horse, get on a rocking horse. If you're a teacher, become a student. If you have graduated, enroll again. If you have completed your term of duty, reenlist. If you have grown old and crusty, let your youth be renewed like the eagles (Psalm 103:5). Become a babe and a fresh revelation of Christ will come in and flood your soul like never before.

August 22
Read: Psalms 49-52; Luke 11

Psalm 51:17
"The sacrifices of God are a broken spirit: a broken and a contrite heart, O God, thou wilt not despise."

We consider something broken to be useless; God declares that when we are unbroken, we are useless.

August 23
Read: Psalms 53-58; Luke 12

Luke 12:49
"I am come to send fire on the earth; and what will I, if it be already kindled?"

The NKJV says this verse with more clarity. *"I came to send fire on the earth, how I wish it were already kindled."* What Jesus is saying is that the fire will be kindled at a later day. What day would that be? The day of Pentecost. That is the day the church received the baptism of the Holy Ghost and FIRE. We are called to be salt and light to this world. How often have you heard you are to be fire? Well, that is what you are to be, so let it be kindled, let it burn.

August 24
Read: Psalms 59-65; Luke 13

Psalm 63:8
"My soul followeth hard after thee: thy right hand upholdeth me."

You can follow hard after God or you can make it hard to follow God. Set your affections on things above and you will follow hard after God; set your affections on things below and it will be hard to follow after God. Let me add, if you do chase after God, He will let you catch Him.

August 25
Read: Psalms 66-70; Luke 14

Luke 14:21-22
"So that servant came, and shewed his lord these things. Then the master of the house being angry said to his servant, Go out quickly into the streets and lanes of the city, and bring in hither the poor, and the maimed, and the halt, and the blind. ²²And the servant said, Lord, it is done as thou hast commanded, **and yet there is room**.*"*

The first century church was anticipating the return of the Lord in their day. Here we are almost 2000 years later and we are still anticipating His return. Why such a delay? *"…Yet there is still room."* Any moment now, the last seat could be taken.

August 26
Read: Psalms 71-74; Luke 15-16

Psalm 71:8
"Let my mouth be filled with thy praise and with thy honour all the day."

Some Christians may say that this verse is an exaggeration. Who can praise and honor God all day long? If you know a man who is going to be marrying a virgin who he loves, ask him who is on his mind. Ask the family, who is going on a great vacation in a few days, what their minds are on. Ask young children, a few days before Christmas, what they are thinking about. You can't help but to think about and ponder on that which you are excited about.

August 27
Read: Psalms 75-78; Luke 17

Luke 17:30-32
"Even thus shall it be in the day when the Son of man is revealed. ³¹In that day, he which shall be upon the housetop, and his stuff in the house, let him not come down to take it away: and he that is in the field, let him likewise not return back. ³²Remember Lot's wife."

Jesus associates returning back for your stuff to Lot's wife. Lot's wife didn't look back because she wanted to glimpse on the destruction that was happening to Sodom; she was looking back because that is where her possessions were. She couldn't let go of them in her heart and therefore she couldn't help but to look back with her head. She could not bear the thought of all that she held dear going up in smoke. Saints, everything is going to burn one day; it is best for us all to get all that *"stuff"* out of our hearts right now and leave it behind.

August 28
Read: Psalms 79-83; Luke 18

Luke 18:31-34
"Then he took unto him the twelve, and said unto them, Behold, we go up to Jerusalem, and all things that are written by the prophets concerning the Son of man shall be accomplished. ³²For he shall be delivered unto the Gentiles, and shall be mocked, and spitefully entreated, and spitted on: ³³And they shall scourge him, and put him to death: and the third day he shall rise again. ³⁴And they understood none of these things: and this saying was hid from them, neither knew they the things which were spoken."

Why would Jesus tell His disciples something that they are not going to understand? Why would He tell them something and then hide its meaning from them? It is because there was coming a day when they would understand. *"And they remembered his words,"* (Luke 24:8). With that in mind, you must realize that there are many things you read that you do not yet understand. Maybe today you will understand something you didn't yesterday. Don't get frustrated if you don't get it, for one day you will. For now, live in what you do know.

August 29
Read: Psalms 84-88; Luke 19

Psalm 85:6
"Wilt thou not revive us again: that thy people may rejoice in thee?"

Saints, it is imperative today that we all live in revival, for our sake and the sake of souls. You must pray and seek the face of God until that revival fire burns in your soul. Then God's people will once again rejoice in Him.

August 30
Read: Psalms 89-92; Luke 20

Psalm 89:11
"The heavens are thine, the earth also is thine: as for the world and the fulness thereof, thou hast founded them."

The heavens belong to God and the earth belongs God. Rejoice, Oh saints, that you belong to God.

August 31
Read: Psalms 93-100; Luke 21

Luke 21:28
"And when these things begin to come to pass, then look up, and lift up your heads; for your redemption draweth nigh."

How will you be able to identify those Christians who are aware of the times we live in? Who are those saints who are not moved by the thought of the calamities coming to this world? Who are those sold out ones who have their hearts and minds fixed on the one who saved them, and are looking forward to going to be with Him? They are the ones walking around looking up for their redemption is oh so close.

September

September 1
Read: Psalms 101-104; Luke 22

Luke 22:26
"*But ye shall not be so: but he that is greatest among you, let him be as the younger; and he that is chief, as he that doth serve.*"

If you learn to enjoy serving others, you will never lack opportunity for enjoyment.

September 2
Read: Psalms 105-106; Luke 23

Luke 23:34
"*Then said Jesus, Father, forgive them; for they know not what they do. And they parted his raiment, and cast lots.*"

Jesus' death on the cross made it possible for the Father to forgive us. Jesus' resurrection from the dead empowers us to forgive one another.

September 3
Read: Psalms 107-111; Luke 24

Luke 24:49
"*And, behold, I send the promise of my Father upon you: but tarry ye in the city of Jerusalem, until ye be endued with power from on high.*"

One of the biggest problems we have in the church today is the unwillingness for preachers to say what needs to be said. There is something even worse than that, it is speaking without being endued with power from on high. Jesus didn't want His disciples to speak until they had it. He expects no less from us today.

September 4
Read: Psalms 112-118; John 1

John 1:4
"In him was life; and the life was the light of men."

The light isn't good works or faithful church attendance. The light isn't shouting out the name of Jesus or people seeing you on your knees praying. The light is the life of Christ, and you are light when that life of Christ is seen in you. The more of Him in you, the brighter the light. When a sinner can no longer look you in the eye or peer at you because of the conviction it brings, then you know the light is really beaming. It won't be because you have a condemning attitude, but because God's holiness, righteousness and love will be oozing out of you. His life is the light.

September 5
Read: Psalm 119:1-104; John 2-3

Psalm 119:89
"Forever, O LORD, thy word is settled in heaven."

No one in heaven questions the word. One of the main reason Christians live half-hearted lives is because they have not settled it in their heart that the word is absolutely true. You will find it a lot easier to obey when you are convinced it is true. If you question the word or follow up with a "but," then the word is not settled in your heart as it is settled in heaven. Don't question or dismiss any of the word, let it be settled in your heart.

September 6
Read: Psalms 119:105 – Psalm 124; John 4

John 4:10
"Jesus answered and said unto her, If thou knewest the gift of God, and who it is that saith to thee, Give me to drink; thou wouldest have asked of him, and he would have given thee living water."

Jesus knew the Samaritan woman was a fornicator and he had no problem exposing it in her life. However, when he approached her, He did not come to her with a list of religious rules to obey or with a heart to condemn her, He came offering her living water. Hallelujah! Living water is the answer for every sinner.

September 7
Read: Psalms 125-135; John 5

Psalm 127:3-5
"Lo, children are an heritage of the LORD: and ***the fruit of the womb is his reward.*** *⁴As arrows are in the hand of a mighty man; so are children of the youth. ⁵Happy is the man that hath his quiver full of them: they shall not be ashamed, but they shall speak with the enemies in the gate."*

Years ago my oldest granddaughter Anna spent the night with my wife Joy and I. After Joy and Anna spent some time making a blanket, all three of us went for a walk in the woods down the street from us. I have discovered that children often love the simple things in life like a walk in the woods. The next morning; I made pancakes for Anna; she loves Grandpa's pancakes. I don't know if she really likes them or if she likes that Grandpa makes them for her. Maybe it is both. Anyway, it is these little precious times that make me say to myself, slow down a minute, don't get so caught up in this world that I fail to recognize the blessings I have in my family. Verse three says that *"the fruit of the womb is his reward."* You know, I think I am just going to enjoy my reward.

Extra:
John 5:38-39
*"And ye have not his word abiding in you: for whom he hath sent, him ye believe not. ³⁹****Search the scriptures; for in them ye think ye have eternal life****: and they are they which testify of me."*

You must not love what you know, but love Who you know.

September 8
Read: Psalms 136-142; John 6

John 6:63
*"It is the spirit that quickeneth; the flesh profiteth nothing: the words that I speak unto you, they are **spirit, and they are life**."*

Our words must proceed from the Spirit. The word is the message, the Spirit is the messenger. The word is life and the Spirit administers that life. The word and the Spirit are the one-two punch of powerful evangelism.

September 9
Read: Psalms 143-148; John 7

Psalm 145:3
"*Great is the LORD, and greatly to be praised; and his **greatness is unsearchable**.*"

People that are not born again can only understand the simple basics of the Bible such as, "Thou shall not steal." Even then, they do not understand the depth of that commandment. The only people who can truly understand the word of God are those who are born from above because God's truth is revealed by revelation knowledge not academic study. However, even the Christian is scratching the surface of the greatness and depth of Christ. Christian, do not be frustrated by that. Don't beat yourself up because you seem to know so little about God. God is unsearchable. Our minds could not possibly handle all the knowledge and understanding of God, it would be an overload and complete breakdown. Look at it this way; it would be a huge disappointment if God was so puny that we could know every aspect of Him like you could your husband or wife, or family members. He is unsearchable. That doesn't mean that you don't have the privilege to search Him out, it just means He is too great that even the human eye cannot get a glimpse of His glory.

September 10
Read: Psalms 149–Proverbs 1-3; John 8

John 8:32
"And ye shall know the truth, and the truth shall make you free."

The phrase, *"shall make you free,"* comes from two Greek words, *eleutheroō* and *humas*. *Eleutheroō* means to liberate and exempt. So the truth does these two things, it exempts from the penalty of sin and then it liberates from a continued life of sin. The word *humas* means you. Yes, the truth exempts and liberates YOU. Hallelujah, me too!

September 11
Read: Proverbs 4-7; John 9

Proverbs 7:5
"That they may keep thee from the strange woman, from the stranger which flattereth with her words."

The strange woman is like unto the harlot church of our day who flatters with smooth words. The leaders and pastors of these churches work hard at finding the right words as not to offend or challenge anyone. The message that, "God loves you," which is a true message, is taken to the extreme level and they make everything about fulfilling your good pleasure. It isn't that hard to discern the difference between the message the harlot church preaches and the message the remnant church preaches; one makes it about you, the other makes it about God.

September 12
Read: Proverbs 8-10; John 10

John 10:27
"My sheep hear my voice, and I know them, and they follow me."

It is one thing to be led TO the Lord; it is another thing to be led OF the Lord.

September 13
Read: Proverbs 11-13; John 11

Proverbs 13:8
"The ransom of a man's life are his riches: but the poor heareth not rebuke."

The rich man won't exchange his riches for Christ. The true believer won't exchange his Christ for riches.

September 14
Read: Proverbs 14-16; John 12

Proverbs 14:1
*"Every wise woman buildeth her house: but the foolish **plucketh it down with her hands**."*

Whenever the church fails, you can be sure that it was the hands of man that brought it down. We must let the unfailing hands of God direct our steps. We must let Jesus continue to, *"upon this rock I will build My church."*

September 15
Read: Proverbs 17-19; John 13

John 13:35
"By this shall all men know that ye are my disciples, if ye have love one to another."

This has never changed, though love is growing cold in this generation. Love is still the evidence of true disciples of Christ. Since love is growing cold, disciples should be all the more obvious.

September 16
Read: Proverbs 20-22; John 14

John 14:27
"Peace I leave with you, my peace I give unto you: not as the world giveth, give I unto you. Let not your heart be troubled, neither let it be afraid."

The world's idea of peace is no war and everyone getting along with their neighbor. The world tries to bring forth peace from the outside in; God brings forth peace from the inside out. If people are at peace with God, then they will have peace with one another.

September 17
Read: Proverbs 23-25; John 15

John 15:9
"As the Father hath loved me, so have I loved you: continue ye in my love."

There is not a single one of us who is perfect. We all have just a measure of things, a measure of faith, a measure of the Spirit. But there is one thing that we do have a full measure of, Christ's love for us. HALLELUJAH!!!!!!!!!!

September 18
Read: Proverbs 26-28; John 16

Proverbs 27:17
"Iron sharpeneth iron; so a man sharpeneth the countenance of his friend."

Our swords can be made sharp only when we cooperate and interact with one another, not when we fight against each other. It takes precision to get a good sharp edge, but swinging at each other and banging our swords together just destroys the edge.

September 19
Read: Proverbs 29-31; John 17

Proverbs 30:15-16
"The horseleach hath two daughters, crying, Give, give. There are three things that are never satisfied, yea, four things say not, It is enough: ¹⁶The grave; and the barren womb; the earth that is not filled with water; **and the fire that saith not, It is enough.***"*

John the Baptist said there is one coming after him who will baptize us in the Holy Ghost and fire. This baptism of fire means a couple things: a fire that refines us, and a fire that makes us zealous for God. So with that said, I pray that we all have that fire that says I can't get enough, I want more of God.

September 20
Read: Ecclesiastes 1-3; John 18

John 18:19-20
"The high priest then asked Jesus of his disciples, and of his doctrine. ²⁰Jesus answered him, **I spake openly** *to the world; I ever taught in the synagogue, and in the temple, whither the Jews always resort; and in secret have I said nothing."*

Cults are notorious for telling you one thing when they are sharing their religion with you, but then when you join up with them, they tell you something different. It must not be so for Christians. We must always speak openly the truth of this gospel. The secret to the mega / seeker sensitive church is they don't speak the truth openly. They don't tell it like it should be told. I guess it all depends on if you are looking to gather people or if you are looking to save people and strengthen saints.

September 21
Read: Ecclesiastes 4-7; John 19

Ecclesiastes 4:9-12
"Two are better than one; because they have a good reward for their labour. ¹⁰For if they fall, the one will lift up his fellow: but woe to him that is alone when he falleth; for he hath not another to help him up. ¹¹Again, if two lie together, then they have heat: but how can one be warm alone? ¹²And if one prevail against him, two shall withstand him; and a threefold cord is not quickly broken."

I love going to church because I fall down sometimes. Sometimes I get cold. I need someone to pick me up when I fall and warm me up when I am cold. When you are cold, you need to be around fiery people. Those who are independent of the church need one of those gadgets that you can press the button and say, "I have fallen and I can't get up."

September 22
Read: Ecclesiastes 8-12; John 20-21

John 20:17
*"Jesus saith unto her, Touch me not; for I am not yet ascended to my Father: but go to my brethren, and say unto them, I ascend unto **my Father, and your Father;** and **to my God, and your God.**"*

Did you get what Jesus is saying here? His Father is our Father, His God is our God. Jesus is saying we have the same connection and privilege to the Father as He does. How awesome is that! Be encouraged today, my brethren.

September 23
Read: Song of Solomon 1-4; Acts 1

Song of Solomon 2:3
*"As the apple tree among the trees of the wood, so is my beloved among the sons. I sat down under his shadow with great delight, **and his fruit was sweet to my taste.**"*

Fruit is meant for people to eat. Fruit tastes the best when it is fully ripe. When fruit is immature, it has little to offer. Is your fruit sweet when others taste it?

September 24
Read: Song of Solomon 5-8; Acts 2

Acts 2:4
"And they were all filled with the Holy Ghost, and began to speak with other tongues, as the Spirit gave them utterance."

The secret to the power and authority of that early church was that *"they were **ALL** filled with the Holy Ghost."* The name "Holy Ghost" is found ninety times in the New Testament; forty-one of those times He is mentioned in the book of Acts. That speaks loud and clear that a Holy Ghost powered church is what God has ordained to invade this world. It wasn't just for the generation of believers 2,000 years ago, but for this present generation as well. If you downplay the ministry and power of the Holy Ghost, then the opposite results will happen, the world will invade the church.

September 25
Read: Isaiah 1-2; Acts 3-4

Isaiah 1:9
*"Except the LORD of hosts had left unto us a **very small remnant**, we should have been as Sodom, and we should have been like unto Gomorrah."*

Remnant believers can get discouraged, wondering if they are doing anything for the kingdom of God. Remnant saint, be encouraged, you are what is keeping the church from being as Sodom and Gomorrah.

September 26
Read: Isaiah 3-5; Acts 5

Acts 5:17-18
*"Then the high priest rose up, and all they that were with him, (which is the sect of the Sadducees,) and were **filled** with indignation, ⁱ⁸And laid their hands on the apostles, and put them in the common prison."*

The high priest and the Sadducees were filled with indignation. That indignation caused a reaction that resulted in the apostles being put in prison. Brethren, if unredeemed men can be filled with something that causes a reaction, then how much more do we need to be filled with the Spirit who causes even a most powerful reaction.

September 27
Read: Isaiah 6-8; Acts 6

Acts 6:5
*"Then said I, Woe is me! for I am **undone**; because I am a man of unclean lips, and I dwell in the midst of a people of unclean lips: for mine eyes have seen the King, the LORD of hosts."*

*"His lord said unto him, **Well done**, thou good and faithful servant: thou hast been faithful over a few things, I will make thee ruler over many things: enter thou into the joy of thy lord"* (Matthew 25:21).

You will never hear *"well done"* until you have been *"undone."*

September 28
Read: Isaiah 9-11; Acts 7

Isaiah 10:20-22
*"And it shall come to pass in that day, that the remnant of Israel, and such as are escaped of the house of Jacob, shall no more again stay upon him that smote them; but shall stay upon the LORD, the Holy One of Israel, **in truth**. ²¹The remnant shall return, even the remnant of Jacob, unto the mighty God. ²²For though thy people*

Israel be as the sand of the sea, yet a remnant of them shall return: the consumption decreed shall overflow with righteousness."

Hang in there faithful saint of God. Any day now the true remnant church is going to escape from the oppression of the false church who has brought a spirit of slumber and worldliness to the church. Remnant believers are those who have leaned, "U*pon the LORD, the Holy One of Israel,* **in truth**." The truth doesn't just set you free, but it keeps you free.

September 29
Read: Isaiah 12-14; Acts 8

Acts 8:1
"And Saul was consenting unto his death. And at that time there was a great persecution against the church which was at Jerusalem; and they were all scattered abroad throughout the regions of Judaea and Samaria, except the apostles."

The world doesn't persecute the church here in America. Why? Because friends argue sometimes, but they don't persecute one another.

September 30
Read: Isaiah 15-19; Acts 9

Isaiah 17:7
"At that day shall a man look to his Maker, and his eyes shall have respect **to the Holy One of Israel.**"

The phrase, "T*he Holy One of Israel*," is found thirty-one times in the KJV Bible. The prophet Isaiah, is the one who saw the Lord high and lifted up and saw and heard the seraphims cry, "*Holy, holy, holy, is the LORD of hosts....*" That explains why that out of the thirty-one times that the phrase, "*the Holy One of Israel*" is stated, Isaiah accounts for twenty-five of those times. That vision he saw left a lasting impression on him, in such a way that he could not help but to see the holiness of God and it showed up in his writings. Saint, this is how you become a holiness saint, not by outward appearance or by joining the "holiness church," but by humbling yourself before the Lord until you get a glimpse of His holiness. It is then that will you truly walk in holiness. It is then that holy will be what you are. It is then that the holiness church can be a holy church.

October

October 1
Read: Isaiah 20-23; Acts 10

Acts 10:38
"How God anointed Jesus of Nazareth with the Holy Ghost and with power: who went about doing good, and healing all that were oppressed of the devil; for God was with him."

God anointed Jesus with the Holy Ghost and power. God has also anointed us, or let me say, has offered to us His anointing. But that anointing is only for those who are consecrated unto God. Anyway, I started off talking about the anointing so I can share with you what God quietly spoke to my Spirit one morning in prayer. He said it in very brief and simple words to me. He told me that I have been more concerned about the messages I preach than having the anointing." He said it to me in a still small voice but it came across loud and clear. I know this isn't startling revelation I have just shared with you, but God made it so real in my heart. Let's all consecrate ourselves, that we too will be anointed from above. Hallelujah!

October 2
Read: Isaiah 24-27; Acts 11-12

Acts 11:26
"And when he had found him, he brought him unto Antioch. And it came to pass, that a whole year they assembled themselves with the church, and taught much people. And **the disciples were called Christians** *first in Antioch."*

The word "Christian" means a follower of Christ. Those in Antioch noticed that these believers followed Christ. Do people take notice that you follow Christ or do you have to try to convince them you do?

October 3
Read: Isaiah 28-29; Acts 13

Acts 13:8-12
"But Elymas the sorcerer (for so is his name by interpretation) withstood them, seeking to turn away the deputy from the faith. ⁹Then Saul, (who also is called Paul,) filled with the Holy Ghost, set his eyes on him, ¹⁰And said, O full of all subtilty and all mischief, thou child of the devil, thou enemy of all righteousness, wilt thou not cease to pervert the right ways of the Lord? ¹¹And now, behold, the hand of the Lord is upon thee, and thou shalt be blind, not seeing the sun for a season. And immediately there fell on him a mist and a darkness; and he went about seeking some to lead him by the hand. ¹²Then the deputy, when he saw what was done, believed, being astonished at the doctrine of the Lord."

Sometimes someone has to be made blind so another can see.

October 4
Read: Isaiah 30-32; Acts 14

Isaiah 30:10
"Which say to the seers, See not; and to the prophets, Prophesy not unto us right things, speak unto us smooth things, prophesy deceits."

A smooth talker can get people to believe a lie. When they get in the pulpits of our churches, they prepare people to meet the antichrist more than they prepare them to meet Christ.

October 5
Read: Isaiah 33-35; Acts 15

Isaiah 35:3-8
"Strengthen ye the weak hands, and confirm the feeble knees. ⁴Say to them that are of a fearful heart, Be strong, fear not: behold, your God will come with vengeance, even God with a recompence; he will come and save you. ⁵Then the eyes of the blind shall be opened, and the ears of the deaf shall be unstopped. ⁶Then shall the lame man

leap as an hart, and the tongue of the dumb sing: for in the wilderness shall waters break out, and streams in the desert. ⁷And the parched ground shall become a pool, and the thirsty land springs of water: in the habitation of dragons, where each lay, shall be grass with reeds and rushes."

To preach that sinners can be saved from an eternity in the lake of fire is great motive for preaching Christ to the sinner. However, consider what you really bring with that gospel message of Christ when you preach it. With Christ comes strength to the feeble, the fearful will be strong, the blind seeing, the deaf hearing, the lame walking, the dumb speaking and Living Water (Holy Spirit) flooding their soul. These things can and do happen in the physical realm, but I am talking spiritually. The spiritually blind will see Christ, the spiritually deaf will hear His voice, the spiritually lame (those who have been wounded in their heart) will walk, joy will stream from the mouth and the Holy Spirit will come in and spring up in that thirsty soul and they will be satisfied forever. PRAISE THE LORD!

October 6
Read: Isaiah 36-37; Acts 16

Isaiah 37:31
"And the remnant that is escaped of the house of Judah shall again take root downward, and bear fruit upward."

If you are of the remnant believer type who is feeling a little down or discouraged, be encouraged, you will again take root downward and bear fruit upward. God is going to raise up the remnant believers in these last days to be that one body and voice. Hallelujah!

October 7
Read: Isaiah 38-40; Acts 17-18

Acts 17:2
*"And Paul, as his manner was, went in unto them, and three sabbath days reasoned with them **out of the scriptures**."*

We are called to believe the scriptures, not debate them. Paul went to the Jews and reasoned <u>from</u> the scriptures, he did not reason <u>over</u> the scriptures like they are somehow open to debate. He used the scriptures to preach the truth and declared that Jesus is the Christ. When he was done, it was up to the hearers if they wanted to believe the scriptures or not. Too often, believers get caught up arguing their point over the scriptures instead of believing the simple truth of the scriptures. The lost go to hell when the church gets sidetracked with their high minded debates over the scriptures.

October 8
Read: Isaiah 41-43; Acts 19

Acts 19:11
"And God wrought special miracles by the hands of Paul."

What Christians like about this scripture is that it excuses them from having to believe God to do special miracles through them. We can all say that God only did those special things through Paul because he was an apostle. But what about plain ordinary miracles? Do you believe God will do them through you or your brethren? Do you believe God will move powerfully in your church assembly? God uses miracles to get people's attention so they can be preached to. God also does miracles amongst His children because He loves them. Let us pray that God will once again do miracles through His believers.

October 9
Read: Isaiah 44-46; Acts 20

Acts 20:29
"For I know this, that after my departing shall grievous wolves enter in among you, not sparing the flock."

Some pastors are so timid they would dare not call out anyone's name who is discovered to be a wolf. Yet, they don't understand it when they lose the sheep who have become easy prey for wolves in sheep's clothing. Saints, don't rebuke or criticize your pastor or other ministers, who in love, warn the body of Christ of the danger that some people are. Be grateful that they understand that the souls of people are way more important than the people's feelings.

October 10
Read: Isaiah 47-48; Acts 21

Isaiah 48:21
"And they thirsted not when he led them through the deserts: he caused the waters to flow out of the rock for them: he clave the rock also, and the waters gushed out."

God caused the waters to gush out when Israel crossed the wilderness. You can be sure, when you get into those wilderness places, God will give you plenty of water. It will be living water.

October 11
Read: Isaiah 49-51; Acts 22

Isaiah 49:3
"And He said to me, 'You are My servant, O Israel, In whom I will be glorified.'"

No matter how far Israel drifted from God, no matter how backslidden they got, God insisted that they will still glorify God. Same for us church. It matters not if the church has run off in a hundred different directions, it matters not if the church has grown cold and indifferent, God will still have a church that will give Him glory. Are you one of those who will?

October 12
Read: Isaiah 52-55; Acts 23

Acts 23:6-8
"But when Paul perceived that the one part were Sadducees, and the other Pharisees, he cried out in the council, Men and brethren, I am a Pharisee, the son of a Pharisee: of the hope and resurrection of the

*dead I am called in question. ⁷And when he had so said, there arose a dissension between the Pharisees and the Sadducees: and the multitude was divided. ⁸**For the Sadducees say that there is no resurrection**, neither angel, nor spirit: but the Pharisees confess both."*

Didn't Jesus set those Sadducees straight about the resurrection of the dead while he was walking amongst them? But, here they are still promoting their false doctrine. Some people are so stubborn, they want their teachings, they want their religion, they want to believe the way they want to believe, no matter what the Lord and the holy word says. Is there anyone in our generation who will forsake all their teachings and religious ideas for the pure word of God?

October 13
Read: Isaiah 56-58; Acts 24-25

Isaiah 56:10-11
*"His watchmen are blind: they are all ignorant, they are all dumb dogs, they cannot bark; sleeping, lying down, loving to slumber. ¹¹Yea, **they are greedy dogs which can never have enough**, and they are shepherds that cannot understand: they all look to their own way, every one for his gain, from his quarter."*

Some mega church pastors will never have enough people.

October 14
Read: Isaiah 59-61; Acts 26

Acts 26:16
*"But rise, and stand upon thy feet: for I have appeared unto thee for this purpose, to **make thee a minister** and a witness both of these things which thou hast seen, and of those things in the which I will appear unto thee."*

God said He will make Paul a minister. Bible college can't do that, studying to show yourself approved can't do that, someone laying their hands on you and ordaining you can't do that. It is God who calls and makes ministers.

October 15
Read: Isaiah 62-65; Acts 27

Isaiah 63:14
"As a beast goes down into the valley, And the Spirit of the LORD **causes him to rest***, So You lead Your people, To make Yourself a glorious name."*

Thank you Lord, for the wonderful rest we find in You.

October 16
Read: Isaiah 66-Jeremiah 1; Acts 28 – Romans 1

Romans 1:16
"For I am not ashamed of the gospel of Christ: for it is the power of God unto salvation to every one that believeth; **to the Jew first, and also to the Greek***."*

This gospel we preach is not a racist gospel; it is not prejudice against anyone. It speaks to the Jew, and then to the rest of mankind. It works for the Jew who believes and it works for anyone else who will believe. There are those who for some reason, think they have to make the gospel relevant. It is clear God made it relevant already. He did not exclude anyone. We need not try to learn someone's culture and custom, just preach the gospel of Christ, it works for all men.

October 17
Read: Jeremiah 2-3; Romans 2-3

Romans 3:4
"God forbid: yea, **let God be true, but every man a liar; as it is written***, That thou mightest be justified in thy sayings, and mightest overcome when thou art judged."*

When man, who is a liar, reads the word which is true, and believes the word which is true and studies it by the Spirit of truth, that person can then quit being a liar. Hallelujah!

October 18
Read: Jeremiah 4-5; Romans 4-5

Jeremiah 5:14
*"Wherefore thus saith the LORD God of hosts, Because ye speak this word, behold, I will **make my words in thy mouth fire**, and this people wood, and it shall devour them."*

Without fire, the wood will never burn. Our words will never have the fire unless they are His words. It is only when His words are in your mouth that fire comes forth and heaps burning coals of conviction on the hearts of men.

October 19
Read: Jeremiah 6-7; Romans 6- 7

Jeremiah 7:28
*"But thou shalt say unto them, This is a nation that obeyeth not the voice of the LORD their God, nor receiveth correction: **truth is perished**, and is cut off from their mouth."*

Herein lies the reason that our politicians and most Americans can no longer tell the truth. *"This is a nation that obeyeth not the voice of the LORD."* Truth has perished in America because this nation refuses to honor God.

October 20
Read: Jeremiah 8-9; Romans 8

Romans 8:30
*"Moreover whom **He** predestined, these **He** also called; whom **He** called, these **He** also justified; and whom **He** justified, these **He** also glorified."*

Our big heads cause us to try to understand and develop doctrines about predestination and being called and so on. Could it be, believers are trying to read more out of this verse than God intended? To bring this to simple understanding, God is telling us that **He** did it all.

October 21
Read: Jeremiah 10-12; Romans 9-10

Jeremiah 10:21
*"For the pastors are become brutish, and have not sought the LORD: **therefore they shall not prosper**, and all their flocks shall be scattered."*

Pastors who do not seek the Lord, will not have spiritual prosperity and success. Thus they invented the seeker - sensitive, easy believism gospel and found worldly success.

October 22
Read: Jeremiah 13-15; Romans 11-12

Jeremiah 13:23
"Can the Ethiopian change his skin, or the leopard his spots? then may ye also do good, that are accustomed to do evil."

You can't change the Ethiopian's skin, but you can kill the Ethiopian. You can't shave off the leopard's spots, but you can kill the leopard. You may not be able to change your old nature, but you can kill it (reckon it dead).

October 23
Read: Jeremiah 16-17; Romans 13-14

Romans 13:10
"Love worketh no ill to his neighbour: therefore **love is the fulfilling of the law**."

The law of love only has two rules, love God with all your heart, soul, mind and strength, and love your neighbor as yourself. If you don't want to be under the law of love, then you will be under a different law that has a thousand other laws to live by.

October 24
Read: Jeremiah 18-20; Romans 15-16

Jeremiah 18:4
*"And the vessel that he made of clay was **marred** in the hand of the potter: so he **made it again** another vessel, as seemed good to the potter to make it."*

Are you marred? Fear not, God will make you again.

October 25
Read: Jeremiah 21-22; I Corinthians 1-2

I Corinthians 1:20
"Where is the wise? where is the scribe? where is the disputer of this world? hath not God made foolish the wisdom of this world?"

For starters, the wisdom of this world says give up eternal peace and joy to seek after a few trinkets now.

October 26
Read: Jeremiah 23-24; I Corinthians 3-4

Jeremiah 23:29-30
"Is not my word like as a fire? saith the LORD; and like a hammer that breaketh the rock in pieces? ³⁰Therefore, behold, I am against the prophets, saith the LORD, that steal my words every one from his neighbour."

Fire consumes the sinner, but purifies the saint; a hammer will bust up the sinner, but drive truth home in the saint. Whatever way you look at it, the word must be preached. God is against anything that a church will do that takes away dependence on the word of God. If the fire is quenched, both sinner and saint will be devastated. If the head comes off the hammer, nothing will be busted up or driven home. Through Jeremiah God asks the question, is not my word like a fire and a hammer? He did not ask that because He needed to know the answer, He asked it in this way. Don't you know that my word is like a fire and a hammer? As we look around today, we can see that much of what calls itself ministry would answer that question with a resounding NO. They have abandoned the word for the latest Christian best seller and have come to depend on programs and entertainment instead. How about you? Do you believe the word still burns the inner man and breaks up fallow ground? If so, then let the word do its work.

October 27
Read: Jeremiah 25-26; I Corinthians 5-6

Jeremiah 25:3-4
*"From the thirteenth year of Josiah the son of Amon king of Judah, even unto this day, that is the three and twentieth year, the word of the LORD hath come unto me, and I have spoken unto you, **rising early and speaking**; but ye have not hearkened. ⁴And the LORD hath sent unto you all his servants the prophets, **rising early and sending them**; but ye have not hearkened, nor inclined your ear to hear.*

It looked as if these prophets of old were men who were up early seeking the Lord. They also spoke to the people early in the morning. We can learn that it is important to take care of all your spiritual matters before you start your day. This is how your day can get off to a good start.

October 28
Read: Jeremiah 27-28; I Corinthians 7

Jeremiah 29:13
"And ye shall seek me, and find me, when ye shall search for me with all your heart."

Some men have died while seeking a cure for cancer. Others have died seeking the lost treasures in the sea. Some others have died seeking after money. But one thing is certain, if you seek God with all your heart, not just 75%, not 90%, not even 99%, all of you will find Him. That is a promise that you never hear too many people proclaim. It even gets better than that. Once you find Him, there is more of Him to seek. In fact, you could live to 100 years old and the pursuit of God would have just started. He is endless, boundless and there is no end to His depth. Saints, if you really look for Him, He will let you find Him. Hallelujah.

October 29
Read: Jeremiah 29-30; I Corinthians 8-9

I Corinthians 8:3
*"But if any man **love God**, the same is known of him."*

I heard a song on Christian radio that has the words, "Oh, how He loves us." By the way, that phrase is repeated another 18 times in that song. As I was reflecting on the thought that God loves me, I attempted to try to stir up in me an overwhelming excitement over this truth that God loves me. I barely got started thinking about it when another thought came to me. I realized what is more exciting to me is when I experience a deep love for God. Take a moment to reflect on this thought saints, isn't Christianity the most exciting when you have that deep love and desire to know and please God? Isn't that when everything else grows dim? When I married my wife Joy I knew she loved me, but I wanted to marry her because I loved her.

October 30
Read: Jeremiah 31; I Corinthians 10

I Corinthians 10:31
"Whether therefore ye eat, or drink, or whatsoever ye do, do all to the glory of God."

The heavens declare the glory of God. But there is another vessel God has created for the purpose of declaring His glory; that vessel is His church. Yes, we are commissioned to make disciples of all nations; yes, we are commanded to love our enemies, but the greatest reason the church exists is to glorify God. If we can accomplish that, all those other things will be fulfilled as well.

October 31
Read: Jeremiah 32; I Corinthians 11

Jeremiah 32:40
*"And I will make an everlasting covenant with them, that I will not turn away from them, to do them good; but **I will put my fear in their hearts**, that they shall not depart from me."*

You don't hear much about the fear of the Lord these days. It seems somehow that the hyper-grace teachings have nullified any need for the church to fear the Lord. However, fearing the One who can throw a man into an eternal lake of fire, is one way the Lord keeps us from departing from Him. The fear of the Lord is meant for our safety, not for us to be constantly biting our fingernails.

November

November 1
Read: Jeremiah 33-35; I Corinthians 12-13

I Corinthians 12:25-26
*"That there should be no schism in the body; but that the members should have the **same care one for another**. ^{26}And whether one member suffer, **all the members suffer with it**; or one member be honoured, **all the members rejoice with it**."*

It is in the nature of Christ to care for others. If I belong to a fellowship of believers, then there will be many others I can care for. There will also be others who will care for me. Those who are independent of the church, for the most part, only have to care for themselves and their family. If I am committed to a fellowship of believers, I will be there to suffer with those who suffer. I will also rejoice with those who rejoice. So too, will those brethren who are committed to the same fellowship suffer and rejoice with me. Those who are independent of the church will suffer alone and rejoice alone.

November 2
Read: Jeremiah 36-37; I Corinthians 14

I Corinthians 14:12
"Even so ye, forasmuch as ye are zealous of spiritual gifts, seek that ye may excel to the edifying of the church."

Some Christians may say, "I don't need the church to be a Christian." I wonder if those who say such a thing ever think the church may need them. Of course, not in the proud condition they are in, but functioning in the body as God has gifted them to.

November 3
Read: Jeremiah 38-39; I Corinthians 15

I Corinthians 15:45
"And so it is written, The first man Adam was made a living soul; the last Adam was made a quickening spirit."

The devil uses the soul to conquer the spirit. God uses the spirit to conquer the soul.

Extra:
I Corinthians 15:41
"There is one glory of the sun, and another glory of the moon, and another glory of the stars: for one star differeth from another star in glory."

You would never be able to see the moon if it were not for the sun. So too, the only glory that men will ever see from saints is if it is the reflection of the Son of God.

November 4
Read: Jeremiah 40-42; I Corinthians 16 – II Corinthians 1

Jeremiah 42:18-19
*"For thus saith the LORD of hosts, the God of Israel; As mine anger and my fury hath been poured forth upon the inhabitants of Jerusalem; so shall my fury be poured forth upon you, when ye shall enter into Egypt: and ye shall be an execration, and an astonishment, and a curse, and a reproach; and ye shall see this place no more. ¹⁹The LORD hath said concerning you, **O ye remnant of Judah; Go ye not into Egypt**: know certainly that I have admonished you this day."*

King Nebuchadnezzar, when he defeated Jerusalem, left behind a remnant of people to live in the land. Nebuchadnezzar left a man in charge that ended up being murdered. This left the remnant restless and fearful and they started to look toward Egypt for a place of security. You may be one of those remnant Christians who has determined to live for the Lord no matter what lies ahead. Beware, because Egypt is always ready to welcome you; "***Go ye not into Egypt.***" You must keep your hands to the plow, looking neither to the left or right and definitely not looking back.

November 5
Read: Jeremiah 43-45; II Corinthians 2-4

II Corinthians 3:17
"Now the Lord is that Spirit: and where the Spirit of the Lord is, there is liberty."

Bondage is not the demand to keep laws, bondage is the demand to keep laws that you have no ability to keep. Liberty is not the freedom from laws and principles, liberty is the power and desire to keep that which pleases God.

November 6
Read: Jeremiah 46-47; II Corinthians 5-6

II Corinthians 5:4
"For we that are in this tabernacle do groan, being burdened: not for that we would be unclothed, but clothed upon, that mortality might be swallowed up of life."

Typically, Christians try to undo things, they try to undo sin and bondage. In a sense, they try to unclothe themselves. But the answer to our spiritual life is not to take off but to put on. It isn't getting rid of, it is getting more of, more of Christ, that mortality may be swallowed up by life.

November 7
Read: Jeremiah 48; II Corinthians 7-8

II Corinthians 7:9
"Now I rejoice, not that ye were made sorry, but that ye sorrowed to repentance: for ye were made sorry after a godly manner, that ye might receive damage by us in nothing."

Some Christians delight in rebuking other Christians. Some Christians who have a self-righteous spirit can't help but rebuke other Christians. Rebuking surely has its place in the body of Christ, but if it is out of any other motive than love, with hope of bringing forth repentance, then the rebuker needs to be rebuked.

November 8
Read: Jeremiah 49; II Corinthians 9-10

II Corinthians 10:18
"For not he that commendeth himself is approved, but whom the Lord commendeth."

We must constantly guard our hearts from desiring the approval of men at the sake of disapproval from God. It is so easy to fall into that trap. There is an indicator called peace that helps us keep our heart right in this matter. If you have the approval of men but lack peace, then you don't have God's approval. If all men were to hate you for what you say or do, but you have God's approval, then the peace of God will strengthen you against all those who would rail against you. Commend your ways to the Lord and enjoy His peace. David said in the Psalm 34, *"...Seek peace, and pursue it."* Living by God's approval is one great way to seek peace.

November 9
Read: Jeremiah 50; II Corinthians 11

II Corinthians 11:3
"But I fear, lest by any means, as the serpent beguiled Eve through his subtilty, so your minds should be corrupted from the simplicity that is in Christ."

This generation has seen corruption on every level. In our government, in our corporations and financial institutions. We have seen it in our schools and on the streets; but the greatest corruption that has invaded our land is the subtly of being led away from the simple gospel of Jesus Christ. The smart boys of religion have complicated Christianity, and have made it so confusing that

Christians have no choice but to go to these same men to help them maneuver their way through all the mess and complication. What Paul feared happened. Don't let it happen to you.

November 10
Read: Jeremiah 51-52; II Corinthians 12-13

Jeremiah 51:20-24
*"Thou art my battle axe and weapons of war: for **with thee will I break in pieces** the nations, and with thee will I destroy kingdoms; ^{21}And **with thee will I break in pieces** the horse and his rider; and **with thee will I break in pieces** the chariot and his rider; ^{22}With thee also will I break in pieces man and woman; and with thee will I break in pieces old and young; and with thee will I break in pieces the young man and the maid; ^{23}I will also break in pieces with thee the shepherd and his flock; and with thee will I break in pieces the husbandman and his yoke of oxen; and with thee will I break in pieces captains and rulers.* ^{24}And I will render unto Babylon and to all the inhabitants of Chaldea all their evil that they have done in Zion in your sight, saith the LORD."

The only people God can use to break down the forces of hell are those who are of a broken and contrite spirit. You can be the broken one God can use to break others, or your heart and spirit can be the object that God is trying to break in pieces.

November 11
Read: Lamentations 1-2; Galatians 1-2

Galatians 1:8
"But though we, or an angel from heaven, preach any other gospel unto you than that which we have preached unto you, let him be accursed."

Paul uses some strong language when he says that those who preach a different gospel should be accursed. I am not advocating we go on a witch hunt, but many need to consider just how serious it is to preach false doctrine. It seems many believers in our generation are so willing to disregard the false teachings that some bring. This neglect is often done in the name of love. Tell me how is that love, if those who preach false doctrine are in danger of being accursed, and believers just shrug their shoulders about it?

November 12
Read: Lamentations 3-5; Galatians 3-4

Lamentations 3:22-23
*"It is of the LORD'S **mercies** that we are not consumed, because his **compassions** fail not. ²³They are **new every morning**: great is thy faithfulness."*

This is one of the reasons Christians should rise early in the morning to seek the Lord; it is at that time when God's mercies and compassions are being made available. Do you need to be renewed? Every morning there is newness.

November 13
Read: Ezekiel 1-3; Galatians 5-6

Ezekiel 3:23-24
*"Then I arose, and went forth into the plain: and, behold, the glory of the LORD stood there, as the glory which I saw by the river of Chebar: and **I fell on my face**. ²⁴**Then the spirit entered into me, and set me upon my feet**, and spake with me, and said unto me, Go, shut thyself within thine house."*

There is no better way for the Spirit to lift you up then to first fall humbly before the Lord.

November 14
Read: Ezekiel 4-6; Ephesians 1-2

Ephesians 2:13
"But now in Christ Jesus ye who sometimes were far off are made nigh by the blood of Christ."

Before Jesus shed His blood, there was an incredible gap between fallen men and God. The blood took care of that problem. We who have come under the blood, are now able to draw close to God, so close that He can live in us, so close that we can be filled with His Spirit.

November 15
Read: Ezekiel 7-9; Ephesians 3-4

Ephesians 4:24
"And that ye put on the new man, which after God is created in righteousness and true holiness."

It is just as easy for the new man to walk in righteousness as it is for the sinner to commit sin. Therefore, put on the new man.

November 16
Read: Ezekiel 10-12; Ephesians 5-6

Ezekiel 11:5
"And the Spirit of the LORD fell upon me, and said unto me, Speak; Thus saith the LORD; Thus have ye said, O house of Israel: for I know the things that come into your mind, every one of them."

Just as each of us need the blood of Christ to wash our sins away, we need the word of God to wash our thoughts away.

November 17
Read: Ezekiel 13-15; Philippians 1

Philippians 1:4-5
*"Always in every prayer of mine for you all making request with joy, ⁵For your **fellowship in the gospel** from the first day until now."*

True Christian fellowship is one of the greatest pleasures that can be experienced among true believers. Yet there seems to be a lack of fellowship amongst believers. Marking it down on the calendar that there will be fellowship on such and such a day does not constitute true fellowship. Calling for the same age groups to get together, organizing groups of people with shared interests and situations of life, is not true fellowship. Why do we have such a hard time finding true fellowship amongst believers? It is because we have tried to find it through other means. Fellowship will be attained and maintained through the gospel. A love for the gospel is love for God and truth. A love for God produces a love for the saints. A love for saints produces fellowship. Promote the gospel and you will promote true Christian fellowship. It will come naturally.

November 18
Read: Ezekiel 16; Philippians 2

Philippians 2:1-2
"If there be therefore any consolation in Christ, if any comfort of love, if any fellowship of the Spirit, if any bowels and mercies, ²Fulfil ye my joy, that ye be likeminded, having the same love, being of one accord, of one mind."

For Paul's joy to be completed the church needs to be likeminded. Paul isn't asking us to put aside our differences; he is insisting that we have no differences.

November 19
Read: Ezekiel 17-19; Philippians 3-4

Philippians 4:9
*"Those things, which ye have both learned, and received, and heard, and **seen in me**, do: and the God of peace shall be with you."*

Paul's preaching had the one-two punch. He spoke it and he lived it. If the people couldn't understand the words he said, they could see a demonstration of it in Paul's life.

November 20
Read: Ezekiel 20; Colossians 1-2

Colossians 2:2-3
*"That their hearts might be comforted, being knit together in love, and unto all riches of the full assurance of understanding, to the acknowledgement of the **mystery of God**, and of the Father, and of Christ; ³In whom are hid all the **treasures of wisdom and knowledge**."*

Some of the best and most exciting books and movies are those about mysteries and treasure hunting. Saint, be reminded you can do more than read or watch a mystery; you can partake of the mystery of God and watch it unfold right before your eyes. You don't have to read or watch treasure hunts; you can go on your own. Be a detective, be a treasure hunter. All the mystery and treasure you could ever want is found in Christ.

November 21
Read: Ezekiel 21-22; Colossians 3-4

Ezekiel 22:30
"And I sought for a man among them, that should make up the hedge, and stand in the gap before me for the land, that I should not destroy it: but I found none."

If God could have found just one man, (that is better odds than God gave Abraham concerning Sodom), to stand in the gap, that man would have satisfied God's fury. It is amazing the influence one godly man can have on a people, on a nation. Can God find someone today?

November 22
Read: Ezekiel 23; I Thessalonians 1-2

I Thessalonians 1:5
*"For **our gospel** came not unto you in word only, but also in power, and in the Holy Ghost, and in much assurance; as ye know what*

manner of men we were among you for your sake."

Paul called the gospel he preached, *"our gospel."* How could he call the gospel of Christ *"our gospel"* like it was his and his brethren's gospel? I guess when you can preach the gospel with power, you will have the boldness to claim it is the real one. With the power comes the boldness to say, listen to my gospel, feel its power and then try to tell me it is not the real deal. Church, our gospel, the gospel of Christ, is the real one. Hallelujah!

November 23
Read: Ezekiel 24-26; I Thessalonians 3-4

Ezekiel 25:1-4
"The word of the LORD came again unto me, saying, ²Son of man, set thy face against the Ammonites, and prophesy against them; ³And say unto the Ammonites, Hear the word of the Lord GOD; Thus saith the Lord GOD; Because thou saidst, Aha, against my sanctuary, when it was profaned; and against the land of Israel, when it was desolate; and against the house of Judah, when they went into captivity; ⁴Behold, therefore I will deliver thee to the men."

The Ammonites cheered when Israel suffered desolation. Israel may have been backslidden, but make no mistake about it, they were still God's chosen people. Since the Ammonites rejoiced over Israel's broken condition, God put Himself against them. Be patient therefore church, this world rejoices when the church suffers persecution, they sneer when they hear that some high profile Christian is caught in immorality and such. But God is watching, God will rise up against those that hate Christ's church. Let's learn a lesson here as well. Let's not rejoice when God gets even with them; let's grieve over them for the judgment they must soon face. I believe God doesn't take pleasure in having to pour out His wrath.

November 24
Read: Ezekiel 27-28; I Thessalonians 5 – II Thessalonians 1

I Thessalonians 5:19-20
"Quench not the Spirit. ^{20}Despise not prophesyings."

There is not a quicker way to quench the Spirit then by despising the *"Thus saith the Lord."* The Spirit of God blesses wherever the word of God is proclaimed and received.

November 25
Read: Ezekiel 29-31; II Thessalonians 2-3

II Thessalonians 2:9-10
*"Even him, whose coming is after the working of Satan with all power and signs and lying wonders, ^{10}And with all deceivableness of unrighteousness in them that perish; because they **received not the love of the truth**, that they might be saved.*

The safe guard against being deceived is to love the truth.

November 26
Read: Ezekiel 32-33; I Timothy 1-2

I Timothy 2:7
"Whereunto I am ordained a preacher, and an apostle, (I speak the truth in Christ, and lie not;) a teacher of the Gentiles in faith and verity."

In our court systems, it is expected for every witness to put their hand on the Bible and "Swear to tell the truth, the whole truth and nothing but the truth, so help me God." Is it too much to ask that the whole truth be told in the church?

November 27
Read: Ezekiel 34-36; I Timothy 3-4

Ezekiel 36:26
"***A new heart also will I give you***, *and a new spirit will I put within you: and I will take away the stony heart out of your flesh, and I will give you an heart of flesh.*"

When a person is born again they don't get a changed heart, they get a new heart, a heart of flesh that can be changed from glory to glory. A stony heart is unchanging and hard and is impossible to reshape. A heart of flesh is like clay in the hands of the potter. The new heart loves what you didn't love before; the new heart hates what you didn't hate before.

November 28
Read: Ezekiel 37-38; I Timothy 5-6

Ezekiel 37:9
"*Then said he unto me,* ***Prophesy unto the wind****, prophesy, son of man, and say to the wind, Thus saith the Lord GOD; Come from the four winds, O breath, and breathe upon these slain, that they may live.* ^{10}*So I prophesied as he commanded me, and the breath came into them, and they lived, and stood up upon their feet, an exceeding great army.*"

Ezekiel was told to, "*Prophesy unto the wind.*" This prophesying brought life. The answer is still the same today, "*Prophesy unto the wind*", and let the wind of the Spirit blow and life will come to the churches again.

November 29
Read: Ezekiel 39; II Timothy 1-2

II Timothy 1:9
"*Who hath saved us, and called us with an holy calling,* ***not according to our works, but according to his own purpose*** *and grace, which was given us in Christ Jesus before the world began,*"

God's calling in our life is not according to our works, talents and abilities. He may or may not use the talents and abilities we have, that is His decision. Don't allow the insistence of some who say you owe it to God to use your abilities for Him. He may want you to lay them down as a sacrifice unto Him. My wife is a great cook, but I didn't marry her to get her food, I married her to get her love. So too, God wants you, and then He will let you know what you must do for Him.

November 30
Read: Ezekiel 40; II Timothy 3-4

II Timothy 4:2
"***Preach*** *the word; be instant in season, out of season; reprove, rebuke, exhort with all longsuffering and **doctrine*** **(teaching)**."

I have heard it said that there is no difference between preaching and teaching; this I disagree with. Though they are closely linked and overlap each other consider this: Preaching is the power of God unto salvation, teaching is the counsel of God unto maturity. Preaching saves souls, teaching disciples saved souls. Preaching fires up the saints, teaching makes the fire burn thoroughly. Preaching brings conviction, teaching shows practical ways to live out the conviction. Preaching revives, teaching survives. Preaching reveals Christ, teaching walks in Christ.

December

December 1
Read: Ezekiel 41-42; Titus 1-3

Titus 1:3
"But hath in due times manifested his word through preaching, which is committed unto me according to the commandment of God our Saviour."

God has ordained the preaching of His word by Spirit-filled believers to be the main method of manifesting His word. There is a saying today, that I totally disagree with, that says the message is the same but the method has changed. Saints, don't fall for that one. Yes, the message is the same but so is the method. Those who believe the method has changed now use drama, entertainment, pep talks and motivational speeches to try to deliver the truth of the gospel. But in due time God, *"manifested His word through preaching."* It still is due time. God committed His word unto us. Therefore, if God has committed His gospel to us then we too, like Paul, are obligated to preach it. Yes, preach it. Faith still comes by hearing.

December 2
Read: Ezekiel 43-44; Philemon - Hebrews 2

Ezekiel 44:4-5
"Then brought he me the way of the north gate before the house: and I looked, and, behold, the glory of the LORD filled the house of the LORD: and I fell upon my face. ⁵And the LORD said unto me, Son of man, mark well, and behold with thine eyes, and hear with thine ears all that I say unto thee concerning all the ordinances of the house of the LORD, and all the laws thereof; and **mark well the entering in of the house***, with every going forth of the sanctuary."*

In the days of Ezekiel, it was a concern of God who it was that came into the temple and what their spiritual condition was. To me it seems the church today is so flippant on just who comes into our churches. In many places it is, "Come one, come all, come as you are and leave as you were." Please understand that I am not against a sinner coming to check out your church, but we need to get back to understanding that the church is a place where holy people meet and that the prevailing attitude is one of worship toward a holy God. The more we disregard holiness, the more the standard of our churches will deteriorate until we do not pay much attention anymore to who it is that attends our churches. The begging and tricking that goes on today to get people to come into our churches has lowered the standard to such a point that the unrighteous feel downright comfortable, and if this is not corrected it won't be long and the devil himself could show up. By then it may be too late for anyone to notice.

December 3
Read: Ezekiel 45-46; Hebrews 3-4

Hebrews 3:13
*"But **exhort one another daily**, while it is called Today; lest any of you be hardened through the deceitfulness of sin."*

It is pretty hard for the casual church attendee to exhort others daily, or be exhorted daily by his brethren, if he does not get together with the brethren. To exhort or be exhorted daily, you must be among the brethren daily for such to happen. That does not necessarily mean that you have to be in the typical church service, but at the least it means to be in daily fellowship with believers. This is how the early church started out, by meeting daily either in the temple or from house to house, in one accord. I have told my church often that I believe the day is coming when we will be meeting most, if not every day of the week. With that in mind, if I am supposed to exhort and be exhorted daily by my brethren, I am going to make it a priority to be with not just any professing Christians, but with those who have a deep love for God and those who have love one for another.

December 4
Read: Ezekiel 47-48; Hebrews 5-6

Ezekiel 47:3-5
*"And when the man that had the line in his hand went forth eastward, he measured a thousand cubits, and he brought me through the waters; the waters were to the **ankles**. ⁴Again he measured a thousand, and brought me through the waters; the waters were to the **knees**. Again he measured a thousand, and brought me through; the waters were to the **loins**. ⁵Afterward he measured a thousand; and **it was a river that I could not pass over**: for the waters were risen, waters to swim in, a river that could not be passed over."*

When you are in ankle deep water, you still can get your own footing. But when you are in the deep water, you can no longer get any footing. The deeper you go, the lighter your body is, until your feet lose all contact with the earth beneath. Saints, get in the flow of the river of the Holy Ghost and lose contact with this earth and let Him take you where He wants.

December 5
Read: Daniel 1-2; Hebrews 7-8

Daniel 2:10
*"The Chaldeans answered before the king, and said, **There is not a man upon the earth** that can shew the king's matter: therefore there is no king, lord, nor ruler, that asked such things at any magician, or astrologer, or Chaldean."*

When, "T*here is not a man upon the earth*" that has the answer you need, that is when the God of heaven will reveal Himself and give the answer you need, if you look to Him.

December 6
Read: Daniel 3; Hebrews 9-10

Hebrews 9:14
"How much more shall the blood of Christ, who through the eternal Spirit offered himself without spot to God, purge your conscience from dead works to serve the living God?"

The blood of Jesus Christ purges and soothes our conscience so we do not have to feel the guilt of past sins. That is one of the amazing things I discovered when I was saved. I was delivered from a guilty conscience. No more guilt, no more feeling of separation from God. Now my works are real and full of life because of the blood.

December 7
Read: Daniel 4; Hebrews 11

Hebrews 11:1-2
*"Now faith is the substance of things hoped for, the evidence of things not seen. ²For by it the elders **obtained a good report**."*

Though our faith requires we believe in God whom we cannot see, our faith in God is must be seen by others. To have *"obtained a good report"* means that others have to see your faith. Faith is way more visible then many people think.

December 8
Read: Daniel 5-6; Hebrews 12

Daniel 5:7-8
*"The king cried aloud to bring in the astrologers, the Chaldeans, and the soothsayers. And the king spake, and said to the wise men of Babylon, Whosoever shall read this writing, and shew me the interpretation thereof, shall be clothed with scarlet, and have a chain of gold about his neck, and shall be the third ruler in the kingdom. ⁸Then came in all the king's wise men: **but they could not read the writing, nor make known to the king the interpretation thereof**."*

It is reserved for those who are born from above who understand that which is written from above. Saint of God, do you understand how privileged you are? It has been given to you to understand the word of God. Take the utmost advantage of that and read it, digest it and let it change your life.

December 9
Read: Daniel 7-8; Hebrews 13 – James 1

James 1:22
"But be ye doers of the word, and not hearers only, deceiving your own selves."

Christians, can at times, get deceived by the tactics of the devil. However, a person doesn't turn to hypocrisy because they get deceived, deception comes to those who play the hypocrite.

December 10
Read: Daniel 9-10; James 2

Daniel 10:19
*"And said, O man greatly beloved, fear not: peace be unto thee, be strong, yea, be strong. And when **he had spoken unto me, I was strengthened**, and said, Let my lord speak; for thou hast strengthened me."*

You can get strengthened every day. All you have to do is open your word and let God speak to you.

December 11
Read: Daniel 11; James 3-4

James 4:10
"Humble yourselves in the sight of the Lord, and he shall lift you up."

It is a hard thing for men to stand up before others and admit their failures, frailties and most of all their sinfulness. Yet, you will find people who will humble themselves before a whole congregation and admit they are sinners. Yet, many of those same people leave the church just as lost as they were when they came in. How can that be, they were so humble? The answer is clear, though they humbled themselves before man, they never humbled themselves before God. When people get in a pinch, they are often willing to beg and cry the blues, which can be awfully embarrassing. Yet when it comes to God the masses will harden their heart. James is a constant reminder to us of our need to be humble and remain humble. More likely than not, if you are feeling down, it is because you have lost a degree of your humility. If you want to live an upbeat life, then a humble and contrite spirit is the answer for you.

December 12
Read: Daniel 12 – Hosea 1-2; James 5 - I Peter 1

James 5:10-11
"Take, my brethren, the prophets, who have spoken in the name of the Lord, for an example of suffering affliction, and of patience. ¹¹Behold, we count them happy which endure. Ye have heard of the patience of Job, and **have seen the end** *of the Lord; that the Lord is very pitiful, and of tender mercy."*

Some Christians never see the pity and mercy of God in their life because they bail out on Him before they get to the end of the trial where the mercy shows up. At the end of trials is where God's tender mercy is magnified.

December 13
Read: Hosea 3-6; I Peter 2-3

I Peter 2:9
"But ye are a **chosen generation**, *a royal priesthood, an* **holy nation**, *a peculiar people; that ye should shew forth the praises of him who hath called you out of darkness into his marvellous light:"*

It is terrible to be prejudice. Yet, God is in a way. He is not prejudice because whoever calls on Him can be saved; that includes every nation, tribe and tongue. However, when it comes to who goes to heaven, it is then He excludes all who are not a chosen generation and a holy nation. It is only those who have Christ in them who will get to go to heaven. If you have not yet called on the Lord to save you, do it while there is still time.

December 14
Read: Hosea 7-10; I Peter 4-5

Hosea 9:14
"Give them, O LORD: what wilt thou give? give them a miscarrying womb and dry breasts."

When a womb miscarries there is no life, when the breasts dry up there is no sustenance. The church does not need an evangelism program, she just needs to be healthy again. Her womb needs to produce life again and her breasts need to put forth plenty of milk (milk of the word). Life begets life, healthy sheep beget healthy sheep. Pastor, FEED THE SHEEP!!!!

December 15
Read: Hosea 11 - Joel 1; II Peter 1

Joel 1:12
"The vine is dried up, and the fig tree languisheth; the pomegranate tree, the palm tree also, and the apple tree, even all the trees of the field, are withered: **because joy is withered away from the sons of men.**"

One of the greatest indicators that the church has dried up and withered is the lack of joy amongst the saints. When I was a Catholic, I was under the impression that a sad face and somber attitude was what God expects from us. But according to my Bible and yours too, the kingdom of God is "...*righteousness, and peace, and JOY in the Holy Ghost*" (Romans 14:17). The lack of joy is the result of dried and withered religion, a religion without the Spirit of God.

December 16
Read: Joel 2-3; II Peter 2-3

II Peter 3:16
"As also in all his epistles, speaking in them of these things; in which are some things hard to be understood, which they that are unlearned and unstable wrest, as they do also the other scriptures, **unto their own destruction.***"*

Christians are not the only ones who use the Bible. Unlearned and unstable people use the Bible as well. For the Christians who love God, the Bible leads them to life, peace and heaven; for those who love mammon and self, it leads them to destruction. God fearing Christians let the Bible lead them, God-resisters use the Bible to their destruction.

December 17
Read: Amos 1-4; I John 1-2

Amos 3:3
"Can two walk together, except they be agreed?"

Considering the lack of unity in the body of Christ, it looks as if no one ever quite answered this question. The answer is NO! Two cannot walk together except they agree. They may be able to walk together physically but they cannot walk together spiritually. Same thing with God, we cannot walk with Him unless there is agreement. But mark it down saints, it won't be a mutual agreement where God agrees with us and we agree with Him. It can be only one way, we must agree with Him. So when you really break it down, much of the church doesn't agree with one another because much of the church doesn't really agree with God.

Extra:
I John 2:20

"But ye have an unction from the Holy One, and ye know all things."

That unction is the Spirit of truth that lives in you. And because the Spirit of truth lives in you, you know all things, even if you don't know it yet.

December 18
Read: Amos 5-9; I John 3-4

I John 4:6
"We are of God: he that knoweth God heareth us; he that is not of God heareth not us. Hereby know we the spirit of truth, and the spirit of error."

Truth is the language all true believers understand.

December 19
Read: Obadiah 1 - Jonah 1-4; I John 5 - II John

Jonah 1:6
"So the shipmaster came to him, and said unto him, **What meanest thou, O sleeper**? *arise, call upon thy God, if so be that God will think upon us, that we perish not."*

The only man on the ship who knew God was Jonah. The only ones in this world who know God is the church. Jonah was sleeping as the sailors were about to perish, the church sleeps as this world perishes. Some may think that the church is very busy accomplishing a lot of things in this world, but to me it looks like they are just sleep-walking. A sleep-walker gets out of bed and walks around. Sometimes they even talk, but they really have no objective. They have no sense of where they are going, they just walk around unconscious of their surroundings. We can make ourselves physically available to the Lord, but it isn't until we are quickened with the burden of the Lord that we will fully rise out of our sleep mode and accomplish a work that snatches the perishing from their path of self-destruction. Wake up, Oh sleeping church.

December 20
Read: Micah 1-3; III John – Jude

Jude 1:21-22
*"Keep yourselves in the love of God, looking for the mercy of our Lord Jesus Christ unto eternal life. ²²And **of some have compassion**, making a difference."*

Having the love of God will result in us acting with the compassion of God. God's compassion is different than man's compassion. Human compassion often results in human effort. When a man is moved by human compassion, his attempt to be a remedy will be by human means. When a man is moved with God's compassion, God will use man, but the remedy will be of God and will glorify God.

December 21
Read: Micah 4-7; Revelation 1-2

Revelation 2:2
*"I know thy works, and thy labour, and thy patience, and how thou canst not bear them which are evil: and thou hast **tried** them which say they are apostles, and are not, and hast found them liars."*

When I think of the church in Ephesus, what often comes to my mind is the church who lost her first love. But Jesus did commend the Ephesian believers for some things they had right. One of those was they *"tried,"* which means they tested self-proclaimed apostles to see if they really were apostles and they found them not to be. Sad to say that today, when a serious Christian wants to test someone to see if they are what they say they are, they are warned to be careful not to touch the Lord's anointed or they are accused of being judgmental. Well, we are to judge the church and not just take the word of every person who claims to be a Christian or a minister. In fact, I expect the saints in the church I pastor to test me, for I test them as well. What is our test? It is the word of God. Who does the teaching? The Holy Spirit. Who sees the grade? People! There is no hiding the test results; they are for the world to see. How well do you score?

December 22
Read: Naham 1-3; Revelation 3-4

Revelation 3:18
*"I counsel thee to buy of me gold tried in the fire, that thou mayest be rich; and white raiment, that thou mayest be clothed, and that the shame of thy nakedness do not appear; and **anoint thine eyes with eyesalve**, that thou mayest see."*

Eyesalve does no good unless you put it on. In other words, you will not see spiritual things unless you desire to.

December 23
Read: Habakkuk 1-3; Revelation 5-6

Habakkuk 2:2
"And the LORD answered me, and said, Write the vision, and make it plain upon tables, that he may run that readeth it."

I am sure most of you heard it said by someone, somewhere along the line, that the reason they don't take the Bible serious or trust it or believe it, is because it was just written by man. Next time you are presented with that argument, here is what you do. Give them a piece of paper and a pen. Then tell them to write down what you say. Then articulate out loud a sentence or a statement. Make sure they write it down. Now ask them who wrote it; they will have to acknowledge that they did. Then ask them whose word it is; they will have to acknowledge that it is yours. The obvious conclusion is that men therefore can write down God's word as well. That should settle that argument.

December 24
Read: Zephaniah 1-3; Revelation 7-8

Zephaniah 3:13
*"The remnant of Israel shall not do iniquity, nor speak lies; neither shall a deceitful tongue be found in their mouth: **for they shall feed and lie down, and none shall make them afraid**."*

Remnant believers love the word of God. Once they feed on it and receive from it, they have rest, even in the midst of a busy day. No trouble in our nation and no devil from hell can make them afraid.

December 25
Read: Haggai 1-2 – Zechariah 1; Revelation 9-10

Haggai 1:14
*"And **the LORD stirred up the spirit** of Zerubbabel the son of Shealtiel, governor of Judah, **and the spirit** of Joshua the son of Josedech, the high priest, **and the spirit** of all the remnant of the people; and they came and did work in the house of the LORD of hosts, their God."*

No work is a true work of God unless it is stirred up by the Holy Spirit.

December 26
Read: Zechariah 2-5; Revelation 11-12

Zechariah 4:6
"Then he answered and spake unto me, saying, This is the word of the LORD unto Zerubbabel, saying, Not by might, nor by power, but by my spirit, saith the LORD of hosts."

Quote from Wesley L. Duewel: "There is no substitute for the power of God. There is no substitute for the Throne of Grace. We dare not be busier than we are blessed. We dare not attempt more than we can saturate with prayer. We dare not be more active than we are anointed. We dare not substitute our training or our brilliance for fire touched glory. We dare not be satisfied with growth without revival. We dare not multiply our projects unless we also multiply the power."

December 27
Read: Zechariah 6-8; Revelation 13-14

Revelation 14:13
"And I heard a voice from heaven saying unto me, Write, Blessed are the dead which die in the Lord from henceforth: Yea, saith the Spirit, that they may rest from their labours; and their works do follow them."

Sometimes Christians fear death too much. They fight so hard against being able to, *"rest from their labours."*

December 28
Read: Zechariah 9-11; Revelation 15-16

Revelation 15:1
*"And I saw another sign in heaven, great and marvellous, seven angels having the seven last plagues; for in them is **filled up the wrath of God**."*

"Filled up" means to be complete or come to conclusion. So with that in mind I say, God's love is eternal, it continues on; God's wrath does have an end. Hallelujah!

December 29
Read: Zechariah 12-14; Revelation 17-18

Revelation 17:1-4
"And there came one of the seven angels which had the seven vials, and talked with me, saying unto me, Come hither; I will shew unto thee the judgment of the great whore that sitteth upon many waters: ²With whom the kings of the earth have committed fornication, and the inhabitants of the earth have been made drunk with the wine of her fornication. ³So he carried me away in the spirit into the wilderness: and I saw a woman sit upon a scarlet coloured beast, full of names of blasphemy, having seven heads and ten horns. ⁴And the woman was arrayed in purple and scarlet colour, and decked

with gold and precious stones and pearls, having a golden cup in her hand full of abominations and filthiness of her fornication."

The harlot church of our day is growing. Her grand finale will be when she becomes the one world religion of the tribulation period. By then the whole world will be given over to her fornications. They will be impressed with her royal purple and scarlet colors, they will trust in her gold, precious stones and pearls. Yes, she looks glamourous, but her path is the way to hell. If you remain with the present day harlot church system, you are setting yourself up for the most powerful of deceptions.

December 30
Read: Malachi 1-2; Revelation 19-20

Revelation 19:1
"And after these things I heard a great voice of much people in heaven, saying, Alleluia; Salvation, and glory, and honour, and power, unto the Lord our God."

John heard the voices of people from a time yet to come. He heard the voices of all the raptured saints. Did He hear your voice?

December 31
Read: Malachi 3-4, Revelation 21-22

Malachi 3:18
"Then shall ye return, and discern between the righteous and the wicked, between him that serveth God and him that serveth him not."

It is expected of the church as a whole to make a clear distinction between herself and the world. If the church cannot discern between the righteous and the wicked, they will certainly not be able to identify those who serve God and those who don't. If the church doesn't know the difference, no one will. Today there is a, "we are all one big happy family" attitude. No standards, no conviction, no holiness, just find the particular fellowship that tickles your fancy. A "don't judge me, I won't judge you" agreement. This prevailing attitude has engulfed much of what calls herself the church and leaves the church without distinction. Saint, you don't have to accept or blend in with that carnal church. Stand firm, be bold and come out from among her, and let that distinction start with you.

For more copies of this book please contact Terry Fischer by email.
pastorfischer@thechurchinwisconsin.com

Made in United States
North Haven, CT
07 May 2022